- chalchica -
- Indica -

Empower →

More Quality —— Less Problems   Japan market
More C.S. —   More Q. — Show
Cost less —   Less Cost = Contact
                                 Don't have to lower price
                                             INFO, SHARING

More Educate the customer — ☐

More Sales

=1 Rory - want to talk to customer
         → Educate -
              → sell ——

Creating
Customers for Life

Management Master Series

William F. Christopher
Editor in Chief

Set 3: Customer Focus

Karl Albrecht
Delivering Customer Value: It's Everyone's Job

Robert King
Designing Products and Services That Customers Want

Wayne A. Little
Shared Expectations: Sustaining Customer Relationships

Gerald A. Michaelson
Building Bridges to Customers

Eberhard E. Scheuing
Creating Customers for Life

Ron Zemke
Service Recovery: Fixing Broken Customers

Creating
Customers for Life

Eberhard E. Scheuing

PRODUCTIVITY PRESS
Portland, Oregon

Management Master Series
William F. Christopher, Editor in Chief
Copyright © 1995 by Productivity Press, Inc.

Productivity Press
P.O. Box 13390
Portland, OR 97213-0390
United States of America
Telephone: 503-235-0600
Telefax: 503-235-0909
E-mail: staff@ppress.com

Book design by William Stanton
Cover illustration by Paul Zwolak
Graphics and composition by Rohani Design, Edmonds, Washington
Printed and bound by Data Reproductions Corporation in the United
    States of America

Library of Congress Cataloging-in-Publication Data
Scheuing, Eberhard E. (Eberhard Eugen), 1939–
        Creating customers for life / Eberhard E. Scheuing.
            p.   cm. -- (Management master series)
        Includes bibliographical references.
        ISBN 1-56327-146-X (hardcover)
        ISBN 1-56327-093-5 (paperback)
        1. Customer relations. 2. Customer services. 3. Consumer satis-
    faction. I. Title. II. Series.
    HF5415.5.S44 1995
    658.8' 12--dc20   95-12449
                                                                            CIP

00 99 98 97 96 95 10 9 8 7 6 5 4 3 2 1

—CONTENTS—

PUBLISHER'S MESSAGE

The *Management Master Series* was designed to discover and disseminate to you the world's best concepts, principles, and current practices in excellent management. We present this information in a concise and easy-to-use format to provide you with the tools and techniques you need to stay abreast of this rapidly accelerating world of ideas.

World class competitiveness requires managers today to be thoroughly informed about how and what other internationally successful managers are doing. What works? What doesn't? and Why?

Management is often considered a "neglected art." It is not possible to know how to manage before you are made a manager. But once you become a manager you are expected to know how to manage and to do it well, right from the start.

One result of this neglect in management training has been managers who rely on control rather than creativity. Certainly, managers in this century have shown a distinct neglect of workers as creative human beings. The idea that employees are an organization's most valuable asset is still very new. How managers can inspire and direct the creativity and intelligence of everyone involved in the work of an organization has only begun to emerge.

Perhaps if we consider management as a "science" the task of learning how to manage well will be easier. A scientist begins with an hypothesis and then runs experiments to observe whether the hypothesis is correct. Scientists depend on detailed notes about the experiment—the timing, the ingredients, the amounts—and carefully record all results as they test new hypotheses. Certain things come to be known by this method; for instance, that water always consists of one part oxygen and two parts hydrogen.

We as managers must learn from our experience and from the experience of others. The scientific approach provides a model for learning. Science begins with vision and desired outcomes, and achieves its purpose through observation, experiment, and analysis of precisely recorded results. And then what is newly discovered is shared so that each person's research will build on the work of others.

Our organizations, however, rarely provide the time for learning or experimentation. As a manager, you need information from those who have already experimented and learned and recorded their results. You need it in brief, clear, and detailed form so that you can apply it immediately.

It is our purpose to help you confront the difficult task of managing in these turbulent times. As the shape of leadership changes, the *Management Master Series* will continue to bring you the best learning available to support your own increasing artistry in the evolving science of management.

We at Productivity Press are grateful to William F. Christopher and our staff of editors who have searched out those masters with the knowledge, experience, and ability to write concisely and completely on excellence in management practice. We wish also to thank the individual volume authors; Diane Asay, project manager; Julie Zinkus, manuscript editor; Karen Jones, managing editor; Lisa Hoberg and Mary Junewick, editorial support; Bill Stanton, design and production management; Susan Swanson, production coordination; Rohani Design, graphics, page design, and composition.

Norman Bodek
Publisher

INTRODUCTION

Customers are the lifeblood of any organization. They inspire everyone with meaning and purpose. They provide incentive, vitality, and growth. To prosper, an organization must choose, nurture, and cultivate its customers carefully. Achieving these goals requires a customer-focused culture and customer-friendly systems. And it requires unrelenting effort toward continuous improvement. But the rewards are well worth the effort: unflinching customer loyalty, sustainable growth, and impressive performance.

Follow the patient
doctor even if the best interest of the ~~doctor~~
or not.

1

THE NATURE AND ROLE OF CUSTOMERS

Customers are essential links in value chains and powerfully determine their success. They are valuable resources and vital assets to the future growth of an organization. For maximum benefit to both sides, a company must manage customers' experiences and behavior with great care.

THE ROLE OF CUSTOMERS IN VALUE CHAINS

A *value chain* is a series of players involved in a process that creates value. Figure 1 shows their relationships.

The players are interactive and interdependent links who collectively produce value to satisfy the requirements of the ultimate link—the external customer. Toward this end, internal and external suppliers contribute inputs that an organization combines into a product offered to external customers.

Customers are individuals or groups of people who depend on a supplier's performance for the success of their own efforts or the satisfaction of specific requirements. *Suppliers* are persons or organizational units that enable customers to succeed in their efforts or gain satisfaction of their requirements. As Figure 1 shows, both customers and suppliers can be either external or internal to an

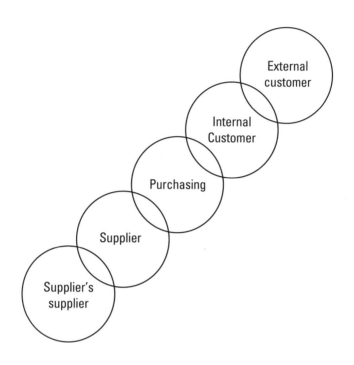

Figure 1. Supplier/Customer Links in Value Chains

organization. They strongly depend on each other and need to cooperate closely for maximum mutual benefit. Although internal customers play an important role in the value chain, none of the other links would exist without the external customers' ability and willingness to buy the ultimate process outputs. For reasons of convenience and custom, therefore, this book uses the term *customers* to refer to external customers or customers in general.

Who Is the Customer?

Customers are not just passive recipients of process outputs. Rather, they are often driving forces and active players in the process of creating value. They frequently initiate the process through inquiries, requests, or purchases. They may contribute inputs that range from suggestions and specifications to drawings, parts, people, equipment, and funds.

This statement, in fact, brings up the question: Who is the customer when an organization makes a purchase? Is the customer

- the purchaser who places the order?
- the engineer who designed the product?
- the technical expert who wrote the specification?
- the requisitioner who initiates the requisition?
- the manager who signs the requisition?
- the person who actually uses the product?
- the person who issues the check?

As the list highlights, the customer is often more than one person. In *organizational buying*, the group of people who participate in a particular sourcing process are called a buying center or sourcing team. Researchers of buyer behavior have identified a variety of players and roles involved in both organizational and *household buying* processes. The following list explains these roles:

- *Gatekeepers* control the flow of information into the group making the decision.
- *Specifiers* spell out what to buy.
- *Influencers* have an impact on the outcome of the decision.
- *Deciders* make the buying decision.
- *Purchasers* carry out the act of purchasing.
- *Users* actually use or consume the product.
- *Maintainers* service the equipment involved.

- *Disposers* dispose of the residue of the use or consumption process.

With such a variety of players and roles involved in many buying processes, the answer to the question "Who is the customer?" becomes quite complex. This issue is essential because it is impossible to create customers for life if these customers have not been clearly identified. This challenge is made even more difficult by the fact that the perspectives and objectives of the individual players involved in a buying situation frequently differ significantly. For instance, specifiers may describe the perfect product; deciders may authorize the most affordable product; purchasers will look for a good deal; and users often want the product immediately. To arrive at a reasonable solution that is acceptable to all players, conflicting objectives have to be reconciled.

THE VALUE OF CUSTOMERS

The importance of customers is captured extremely well in the French expression *la raison d'etre:* customers are an organization's *reason for being.* Unfortunately, all too many employees in large organizations forget this simple fact and display an attitude that says: "If only those customers would leave us alone, we could get our work done." This kind of attitude is a sign of an inwardly focused, bureaucratic organization that has lost sight of its essential purpose and makes customers adhere to its rules, rather than listening to them and making its systems customer-friendly.

Customers Are Assets

Customers provide an organization's livelihood. Therefore, they can reasonably expect to be appreciated and treated with attention and care. They are valuable assets because they provide streams of revenues and profits that ensure the organization's survival and growth. Customers are also potential sources of new product ideas. After all, they know best what they need or want, and their buying decisions determine whether a new product succeeds.

To build a solid base, an organization must choose and analyze customers carefully. Their characteristics should fit a desired profile, which also is likely to make them compatible with each other. This dimension is important because customers often interact with each other and may well affect each others' experiences and satisfaction. Accordingly, an organization must carefully manage customer behavior to fit a preconceived pattern and produce satisfaction all around—of employees, fellow customers, and the customers themselves.

This may well mean that organizations need not only to select customers, but also to train them. Universities have learned that merely attracting and admitting more students is not the road to unqualified success. Rather, universities need to identify the kinds of students they would like to see enroll in specific programs, then devise approaches to finding and appealing to these target groups. Once they have successfully attracted the desired caliber and mix of students, universities must help these students succeed within their specific frameworks.

In other words, no organization can be all things to all people. Rather, it must examine its core competencies and formulate its desired customer profile based on this assessment. *Core competencies* are the unique characteristics and capabilities that set an organization apart in the marketplace and create its competitive advantage. If an organization manages to attract a compatible customer mix and transform these customers into loyal buyers, this customer base itself can become a source of competitive advantage.

Customers Are Sources of Growth

Customer relations are fragile creations. An organization must carefully nurture and cultivate them to survive the competitive onslaught and the ravages of time. It pays to delight customers, because delighted customers are grateful and order more. In fact, customer delight builds its own momentum as delighted customers not only provide more business, but also spread the word and refer their friends.

A Case in Point

Shouldice Hospital in Toronto, Canada, specializes in correcting inguinal hernias. It does not advertise, but thrives instead on word-of-mouth from former patents, who enthusiastically recommend Shouldice to their friends. Shouldice is also, quite likely, the only hospital in the world that holds "alumni reunions." Every year, some 1,500 former patients fill the Grand Ballroom of the Royal York Hotel in Toronto to capacity to swap hernia stories. The atmosphere is much like that of a meeting of veterans who shared a trench in the war. At most, former patients shared a three-day stay at Shouldice, which practices early ambulation and quick discharge. The reunions are eagerly anticipated social events, and some "alumni" have been attending annually for decades. Needless to say, this unique fan club keeps generating a steady stream of new business.

2

PURSUING EXCELLENCE

In attempting to create customers for life, an organization needs to provide and maintain excellence. But many impediments can get in the way of providing excellent service to customers. Curiously, the very elements that act as barriers can often be used to achieve excellence, provided the organization manages them properly.

THE NATURE OF EXCELLENCE

Excellence can be defined as consistently exceeding customer expectations. The relationship between customer expectations, perception, and response is illustrated in Figure 2.

Expectations are anticipated future conditions. Figure 3 shows that customer expectations can be expressed on a vertical scale that extends from low to high. In between these extremes lies the *normal range*, which extends from barely acceptable to desirable. The barely acceptable level reflects the minimum tolerable performance. The desirable level, in contrast, refers to the kind of performance the organization can and should deliver.

Performance in the normal range results merely in customer satisfaction. The organization has delivered what it promised or can reasonably be anticipated to deliver. Actual performance matched expectations, so the

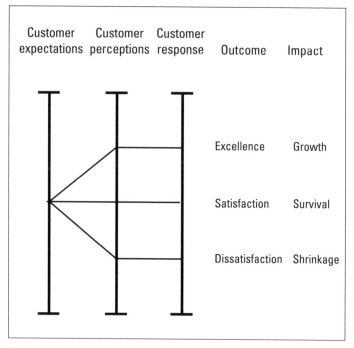

Figure 2. Factors Driving Customer Behavior

organization survives for now. But it remains highly vulnerable to competitive inroads. Competitors who deliver
the same performance for less money or better results for
the same price can readily take business away. After all, the
organization's customers are merely satisfied, not enthused.

The situation is a lot worse if perceived performance
falls short of expectations, particularly below the barely
acceptable level After all, the *mind* of the customer is the
battleground. *Perception* is what customers *think* they
received, not what was actually delivered. If customers
think they were shortchanged, then they were. And that
makes them leave. They defect in droves, and the business

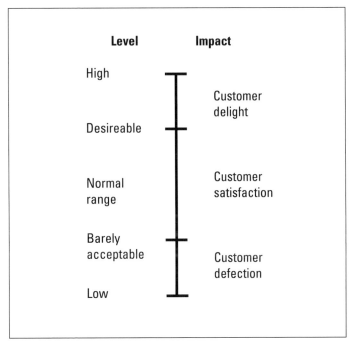

Figure 3. Exploring Expectations

shrinks. Worse yet, they take many potential customers with them.

Complaints Provide Valuable Feedback

Research indicates that for every dissatisfied customer who complains to an organization, 26 other customers are equally dissatisfied, but do not complain to the organization. They tell others, however—in fact, about ten others on average. This negative word-of-mouth discourages potential customers from giving the organization a chance. So, for every complaining customer, possibly 260 others either had a bad experience or heard about one and, thus, won't do business with the organization. But the organization never gets a chance to hear about it and take corrective action.

So it is essential to encourage and welcome complaints instead of treating them as unjustified nagging or evil nuisances. A customer who complains offers an organization a chance to correct an alleged faulty performance or set the record straight by educating the customer about the true nature of the situation. Most customers whose complaints are resolved continue to do business with an organization. If the organization resolves their complaints promptly, they may even become loyal customers.

It helps to ask complaining customers what would make the situation right for them and then surprise them by going beyond what they requested or suggested. Correcting perceived performance problems is known as *recovery*. Recovery requires an appropriate process that enables quick action. It is both an art and a skill. As an art, it involves sensitivity, judgment, and flair. As a skill, it can and must be taught because it is an invaluable means of gaining critical insight and recapturing the goodwill of customers ready to defect.

People Drive Excellence

Of course, instead of trying to prevent defection, every organization should strive to "top the charts" by exceeding the normal range of customer expectations and delighting them. Delighted customers are loyal customers, and they are an organization's best "salespeople." To delight customers, employees need to go the extra mile and surprise them with exceptional performance.

MOMENTS OF TRUTH

The Harvey Hotel in Plano, Texas uses a video entitled *Exceeding Guest Expectations* to encourage this spirit in its employees. The video stars actual colleagues recounting "moments of truth." The concept of a moment of truth was first popularized by Jan Carlzon, the president of Scandinavian Airlines System (SAS), in the early 1980s. A moment of truth is an encounter between an employee of an organization and an actual or potential customer. The encounter may be planned or unplanned, formal or informal. At that moment, however, in the eyes of the customer, the employee *is* the organization. Whatever the employee says or does reflects on the organization as a whole. If the employee mishandles the situation, bitter feelings can result, and the customer may defect. But if the employee shines, the organization shines. At the point and moment of contact, the employee personifies the organization. This is why proper selection, training, and motivation of employees are essential ingredients in the success of any organization.

The Harvey Hotel video reports several instances where front-line employees turned guest encounters into memorable experiences. One bellhop was just bringing a guest to his room in his wheelchair when the fire alarm went off. He carried the guest five flights of stairs to the lobby. Another bellhop, upon learning that a guest's rented car had a flat tire, promptly changed the tire. A waitress realized that a young couple had to cut their dinner short because their daughter was restless She offered to prepare a dessert in their room after hours. None of these instances involve heroic deeds. But in all instances, the employees displayed behaviors that go beyond the ordinary and delight guests because they reflect a caring, can-do attitude.

CREATING LOYAL CUSTOMERS

To create customers for life—customers who demonstrate fervent, unswerving loyalty—an organization needs to achieve excellence on an ongoing basis. It can achieve this only if it continuously instills and reinforces a spirit of customer passion in employees. Stew Leonard's in Norwalk, Connecticut, is such a place. Billing itself as "the world's largest dairy store," this organization is listed in the *Guinness Book of World Records* as having the highest sales per square foot of any store in the world. And it does so by selling the most mundane products, such as eggs, bread, and milk, which can be obtained in millions of stores. So what is its magic? Stew Leonard's offers guaranteed fresh quality merchandise at reasonable prices, but it also makes shopping fun. There is a carnival atmosphere at Stew Leonard's with costumed characters entertaining children, aromas of freshly baked products wafting through the air, and samples being offered at every turn.

What is perhaps most amazing about the success of Stew Leonard's is the fact that the loyalty of its customers has withstood the ultimate test. Stew Leonard, Sr., the store's founder and ebullient cheerleader, is serving a prison term for massive tax evasion. While such unethical and illegal behavior would have been deadly for most organizations, Stew's customers have rallied to continue their patronage of the original store in Norwalk, which his son Stew, Jr., now manages, and a second store in Danbury, Connecticut, which Stew's son Tom manages. Both of his daughters are also active in the family business. Extensive research confirms that 96 percent of Stew Leonard's customers still buy from his organization, which generates $100 million in sales per store per year. They do so because they receive value for their money and exceptional service.

How do the Leonards achieve such indestructible customer loyalty? They may well be the world's best *listeners*. Before shoppers leave either store, they face a large sign asking for their comments and suggestions. At the Danbury store, stacks of sheets bear Tom's picture and the simple invitation "What Do You Like, What Don't You Like? I'd Love To Know! Your Friend, Tom Leonard" to encourage spontaneous written feedback. The company daily processes and acts on the resulting comments and suggestions.

Family members and managers also frequently walk the floor, greeting customers and asking for their opinions and experiences. Regular focus group sessions or round-table discussions with customers round out the picture. And Stew Leonard's takes prompt action. When a customer suggested displaying fresh fish on cracked ice instead of plastic trays with cellophane covers, a fresh fish counter was built the next day, tripling fresh fish sales.

It is hardly a surprise that to achieve exceptional customer loyalty, Stew Leonard's invests substantially in training and rewarding its employees, who are called team members. All new members receive initial training before they assume their responsibilities. Members also attend periodic internal training sessions and external seminars. They nominate each other for awards and receive recognition and rewards for going above and beyond the call of duty (ABCD). They are empowered to do whatever it takes to please a customer and praised for doing so in a process known as "management by appreciation."

BARRIERS TO EXCELLENCE

If excellence is so exciting and rewarding, why is it not widespread? If its benefits are so obvious in terms of customer loyalty and bottom-line performance, why are so few American companies pursuing and receiving the coveted Malcolm Baldrige National Quality Award? After all, the Baldrige Award encourages and recognizes world-class quality, which is merely another word for excellence.

The answer is simple: It is hard to achieve excellence consistently. There is only one Stew Leonard's in the world. And there is only one Nordstrom department store chain, which is legendary for its level of service and commitment to customers.

A lot of barriers can get in the way of excellence. Most of them fall into three categories: systems, people, and strategies. Properly managed, these three elements actually enable organizations to achieve excellence. But when managed inadequately, they become obstacles that prevent excellence. And it is so much easier to manage them poorly or not at all.

Systems as Barriers

Ever since Alfred P. Sloan created functional specialization at General Motors, American organizations have been characterized by vertical structures. Functions such as marketing, purchasing, and finance are distinct and separate from each other, have their own hierarchies, and protect their respective turfs from intrusion by others. Some have referred to these breakdowns as *silos,* to highlight the insular, self-contained nature of traditional functional specialization. Others talk about throwing things "over a wall" to indicate that accountability ("the buck") passes from one function to the next with little cooperation. In fact, such interactions are often characterized by hostility, finger pointing, and rejection.

Experience indicates that customers often become the unwitting victims in such internecine wars. The individual functions suboptimize because their own performances are more important to them than the success of the organization as a whole. Marketing may make promises that the production or operations function cannot keep. Purchasing may follow standard procedures instead of exerting a special effort to meet customer needs. And customer requests or inquiries may be bounced around all over the place because nobody cares to assume responsibility for a problem.

Most systems have been designed to suit the convenience of the organization, not its customers. Patients who are brought to hospital emergency rooms in acute distress may face thorough interrogation about their medical coverage and an extensive wait before they are examined and treated. This apparent lack of concern for their condition, in fact, tends to aggravate it further and is thus clearly counterproductive.

In marked contrast, patients arriving at Shouldice Hospital (who are clearly not experiencing an emergency) are greeted and treated by a smoothly functioning system that considers them valued guests, not unwelcome problems. Every part of their brief stay is designed and choreographed to maximize interaction, ambulation, and enjoyment. All patients have surgery the day after their arrival in a building that otherwise passes for a mansion in a country club setting. Having had only local anesthesia, they are asked to get off the operating table under their own power (with some assistance) and start strolling about the gardens within two hours. Beds are just for sleeping. All patients are up and about all day. They share meals and recreational activities, and are usually discharged within three days.

People as Barriers

It's employees, ultimately, who make or break an organization. Unmotivated employees provide, at best, indifferent service. This fact is perfectly evident in many civil service settings. All too many government workers interacting with the public treat the recipients of their services with a strange mixture of arrogance, lack of concern, and even disdain. They can get away with this kind of behavior as long as the public does not have any alternative to their service.

For instance, procedures at the Immigration and Naturalization Service are very inefficient and frustrating for immigrants. They have to take time off from work and stand in line for an hour just to schedule an appointment to submit an application for a new alien registration card that attests to their status as permanent residents, as granted years ago. They receive a number and approach the designated counter when their number is up. They have to stand, shout their questions through a glass pane in a crowded, noisy room to a person seated comfortably on a chair, only to be treated with impatience and barked commands by the Immigration officer (who speaks only English). Having survived this first ordeal, the immigrants then have to take off time from work again on the designated date and are shocked to find hundreds of other people waiting at the time of the "appointment." This time, the torture may well be extended by having to stand in line repeatedly for photographing, fingerprinting, payment, and application acceptance.

No private sector organization could survive treating its customers this way unless it faced no competition. The quasi-private United States Postal Service operated this way until more nimble competitors started siphoning off its customers. Federal Express and others offer overnight small-package delivery service that USPS has tried to match with its Express Mail service. This kind of vigorous competition has done wonders to transform USPS into a more responsive organization with more service-minded employees.

As for the U.S. government, on September 11, 1993, President Clinton issued Executive Order 12862, entitled "Setting Customer Service Standards." Based on the

National Performance Review, headed by Vice President Al Gore, the order stated that "The Federal Government must be customer-driven. The standard of quality for service provided to the public shall be: Customer service equal to the best in business." The introduction to a report of the National Performance Review, entitled "Putting Customers First: Standards for Serving the American People," released in a White House ceremony, compared the now defunct Military Traffic Management Terminal Service with Federal Express and stated that its initials were interpreted by its customers as "Maybe Today, Maybe Tomorrow, Someday." The report then presented customer service standards for a variety of customer groups.

It is also evident that inadequately trained employees simply cannot excel. New employees are all too often merely shown "how we do things around here." After this perfunctory introduction to the organization and its practices, employees are usually left to their own devices, learning on the job as they go along. If a company doesn't teach employees how to identify customers and understand their expectations, it will be all but impossible for them to meet these expectations, far less exceed them.

Employees simply cannot excel without the proper support systems and tools. They need fingertip access to computerized data bases and the capability to enter and update information instantaneously. State-of-the-art information technology is an essential prerequisite for excellent performance. In a broader sense, the latest equipment, properly serviced and maintained, enables professional service delivery. Federal Express can track packages continuously because its couriers carry scanners that they insert into on-board computers in their delivery vans. This information is, in turn, transmitted to a central station to monitor package movement and delivery. The company equips major customers with terminals that facilitate shipping and tracking, including electronic transmission of receipt signatures.

Strategies as Barriers

Another set of obstacles that can detract from delivering excellence to customers derives from an organization's strategies. Most organizational strategies favor acquiring new customers rather than holding on to existing ones. Salespeople are rewarded for bringing in new business, but usually have little incentive to ensure the satisfaction of current customers. In car dealerships, salespeople earn commissions on car sales and tend to see little merit in helping resolve subsequent service problems.

Also, an organization's rules often get in the way of excellent customer service. Elaborate policies and procedures manuals may restrict employees' ability to act in the customer's best interest. This is why Len Berry, who has studied service quality in the U.S. for more than a decade, fervently suggests to executives to "throw away the rule book" to free employees up to do what is right for the customer.

3

CREATING A PASSION FOR CUSTOMERS

To create customers for life, management must instill and continually reinforce a genuine passion for delighting customers throughout the entire organization. Toward this end, it must present a vision of excellence, champion it, and provide appropriate rewards.

A VISION OF EXCELLENCE

A *vision* is a powerful image of what an organization intends to *become*. In contrast, its *mission* describes its *current state*. A mission statement outlines the uniqueness of the organization or *what* (nature) it proposes to be to *whom* (customers). By painting an inspiring picture of its future condition, a vision statement enables an organization to transition to an improved, more advanced level of performance.

In the early 1980s, IBM stumbled because "Big Blue" did not have a clear vision. The company was mired in its traditional ways, accustomed to dominating its industry and dictating products and terms to its customers. Although its products and services were expensive, IBM had long been the safe choice for its customers. But more aggressive, nimbler competitors had long underpriced and outperformed IBM products and services. Worse yet, its key decision makers did not maintain contact with customers and made decisions without adequate customer input.

Achieving excellence requires a powerful, exciting vision that moves people to act in concern to delight the customer. Management must base this vision on a set of values that are easy to understand and widely practiced. Such values are likely to include honesty and trustworthiness, caring and respect for the dignity of the individual, innovation and creativity, openness and flexibility, and commitment to customer service and continuous improvement.

Focus on People

To be effective, a vision of excellence must focus both on employees and on customers—in that order. To put it simply: happy employees make for happy customers. Happiness is contagious. It spreads quickly. The cornerstone of the success of the Marriott hospitality organization is the motto advanced by its founder J. Willard Marriott: "Take care of the employees and they'll take care of the customers." His son, the current chairman, makes it his business to talk to dishwashers, housekeepers, and other staff members as he visits the company's properties to find out whether they are being treated fairly and their concerns are being addressed.

Hal Rosenbluth, CEO of the Philadelphia-based international travel organization that bears his family's name, entitled his book (coauthored with Diane McFerrin Peters) *The Customer Comes Second (and Other Secrets of Exceptional Service).* In this book, he describes the transformation of a small local travel agency into a significant international operation based on the careful selection and development of all associates. Their commitment and excitement translate into many loyal clients.

CHAMPIONING EXCELLENCE

An organization can achieve and maintain excellence only if it has a relentless, tireless champion. And this champion must be the CEO. Excellence can only come from the top because an organization gets what it rewards, and the chief executive sets and metes out the rewards.

Examples of excellent organizations and their champions abound. Jamie Houghton, chairman and CEO of Corning Incorporated, is a tireless enthusiast who keeps driving his multinational company toward excellence. He emphasizes quality and customer commitment in all of his speeches, makes funding available for appropriate initiatives, and measures performance against ambitious goals. His unrelenting zeal is reflected in the Corning policy, which drives the actions of Corning employees worldwide.

CORNING POLICY STATEMENT

It is the policy of Corning to achieve total quality performance in meeting the requirements of external and internal customers. Total quality performance means understanding who the customer is, what the requirements are, and meeting those requirements, without error, on time, every time.

In a similar manner, Herb Kelleher, founder and CEO of Southwest Airlines, energizes his "crew" with his boundless enthusiasm. In its May 2, 1994 edition, *Fortune* features him in the cover story, entitled "Is Herb Kelleher

America's Best CEO?" It summarizes his personality and achievements on the cover in the following sentence: "He's wild, he's crazy, he's in a tough business—and he has built the most successful airline in the U.S." The article states that "Southwest employees often go out of their way to amuse, surprise, or entertain passengers." No wonder Herb's passengers are fiercely loyal and have made his airline the only one to be consistently profitable over the last twenty years. His passengers have a good time while they fly and his fares are lower than those of his competitors. An unbeatable combination—as his envious competitors have found out.

Actions Drive Excellence

Excellence cannot be achieved by decrees from the corner office. In their bestseller *In Search of Excellence*, Peters and Waterman identified an approach they called "management by wandering around (MBWA)" as a critical ingredient of excellence. Chief executives who follow this philosophy do not isolate or insulate themselves in their executive suites, but stroll around to chat with the employees in their organizations.

If they are able to create an atmosphere of openness, like Roger Hale of Tennant Company in Minneapolis, they can keep their finger on the pulse of their organizations and receive invaluable inputs from front-line employees. Hale frequently walks the plant floor of his motorized floor-sweeper equipment company and chats with workers at their work stations.

If CEOs are able to instill trust in their associates, like Ben Strohecker of Harbor Sweets in Salem, Massachusetts, they achieve levels of commitment that propel their organizations relentlessly. Strohecker, the founder and owner of this small maker of fine custom chocolates, practices "open book management" by sharing financial information with all employees. He also entrusted his company to his employees during a one year leave which he took to render community service. He sums up his experience in the words: "Trust works."

Actions speak louder than words. In fact, lip service is cheap. So genuine commitment to excellence must be modeled. GTE Corporation uses a top-down or cascading approach in instilling its "Quality—The Competitive Edge" philosophy in its worldwide workforce. After they receive the appropriate training, the leaders of each division train their people and practice appropriate behavior to lead by example.

REWARDING EXCELLENCE

Excellent performance cannot, and should not, be expected to be its own reward. Rather, excellence needs to be rewarded. Decades ago, Skinner's experiments indicated that behavior that goes unrewarded will cease. If an organization truly wants to encourage excellence, it must provide appropriate rewards.

Fairfield Inns, a budget motel chain operated by Marriott, has devised a unique, high-tech way of capturing the level of guest satisfaction. At the cashier's window, guests who are ready to check out have access to a screen asking them how satisfied they were with the check-in, room, and other services. While their invoice is being prepared, they can quickly answer these questions. The compensation of individual service performers is linked to these satisfaction ratings because the organization tracks who serves particular guests.

Many telephone companies have long linked managerial and executive compensation to customer satisfaction ratings generated by independent outside agencies from customer interviews. And American Express gives its Best Performer Award to employees who go to unusual lengths to please customers.

Recognition and Celebration Energize Excellence

Recognition involves public praise in front of one's colleagues, usually in an appropriate ceremony. Winning an award for exceptional performance has a great deal of meaning for employees because it publicizes their accomplishments and holds them up as examples to others. Some organizations attach monetary benefits or prizes to an award, others grant temporary or lasting privileges.

Recognition for outstanding performance has greater meaning if the criteria for selection are clear and if the recipients are nominated or even chosen by their peers. Many hotels recognize the "employee of the month" in this manner, post his or her picture in the lobby, and award the winner a reserved parking space for a month. There is considerable controversy as to whether recognition should be given to individuals or only to teams. While the answer to this question depends on the circumstances, one thing is quite clear: Recognition is an effective and efficient way to spur outstanding performance.

A number of leading organizations have gone so far as to pattern their internal award systems after the Baldrige Award. Westinghouse and AT&T are among the companies that use this approach to promote aggressive internal competition for excellence. Reflecting Olympic medals, AT&T has bronze, silver, and gold categories for its teams. In a somewhat ironic twist, its Universal card unit won an internal Chairman's bronze award in the same year that it received the Baldrige Award for world-class quality in services. This attests to the high standards that AT&T and others impose in their recognition programs.

Celebration, finally, adds an element of fun to the never-ending quest for excellence. Having a good time with colleagues at a picnic, gold outing, show, or similar event to celebrate joint efforts to achieve excellence for customers is a neat way to say "thank you" to all and keep up the good spirit.

4

TOOLS FOR ACHIEVING EXCELLENCE

If excellence is such a worthwhile pursuit and exciting challenge, how does an organization achieve it? Figure 5 shows three power tools to use in concert to reach this vital goal.

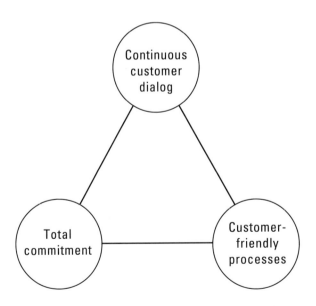

Figure 4. The Excellence Triad

No organization can achieve, or even maintain, excellence without engaging in a continuous dialog with its customers. The very essence of excellence, however, is people and their commitment to superior service. Their efforts, in turn, produce lasting results only if the organization's processes are customer-friendly.

CONTINUOUS CUSTOMER DIALOG

It is no accident that the most important category (300 points or 30 percent) in the Baldrige Award Criteria is "Customer Focus and Satisfaction." The description reads: "The *Customer Focus and Satisfaction* category examines the company's relationships with customers, and its knowledge of customer requirements and of the key quality factors that drive marketplace competitiveness. Also examined are the company's methods to determine customer satisfaction, current trends, and levels of customer satisfaction and retention, and these results relative to competitors."

To achieve excellence and delight its customers, an organization needs to engage in an ongoing dialog with them (see Figure 5).

Traditionally, organizations have practiced one-way communication by using marketing tools to promote their offerings. Excellence and customer delight are all but impossible to achieve in this manner because the organization never knows what the customers' requirements are and whether it has met them. This shortsighted approach leaves an organization highly vulnerable to more sophisticated, customer-focused competitors.

Enlightened organizations, on the other hand, practice closed-loop communications with their customers. Communications flow both ways—frequently, if not continuously. Organizations proactively solicit customer

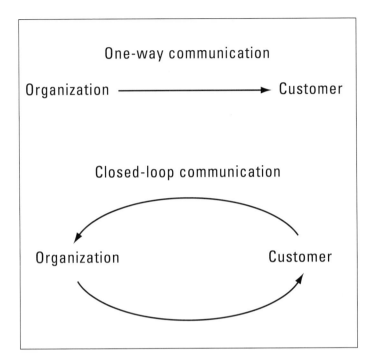

Figure 5. From One-way to Closed-loop Communication

input for the design and redesign of products and services as well as their delivery systems. They ask customers what their needs, expectations, requirements, and even desires are. They encourage customers to offer ideas, comments, and suggestions. They also periodically request customers to provide feedback by rating the performance of the organization as a whole, as well as that of individual employees. This process helps identify and reward employee excellence and pinpoint opportunities for improvement.

Engaging in two-way communications with customers produces another important benefit. The organization learns about the effectiveness of its customer-directed communications and is thus able to close the communications loop. It can also streamline, orchestrate, and fine-tune its communications in line with the feedback it receives from its customers. Also, customers appreciate being asked and being heard. They tend to reward closed-loop communications with loyalty.

Listening to Customers

A variety of tools are available to resourceful leaders eager to tune in to customers:

- **Focus groups.** Roundtable discussions with small customer groups
- **Surveys.** Questionnaire studies of a large number of customers
- **Critical incident reports.** Specific experiences told in customers' own words
- **Advisory panels.** Representative group of customers offering advice
- **One-on-one conversations.** Person-to-person, face-to-face contacts with individual customers

FOCUS GROUPS

These informal roundtable discussions with small groups of customers are facilitated by skilled moderators. Stew Leonard's holds focus group sessions right on the store's premises. The president moderates the discussion as senior executives engage in direct dialog with customers. They ask, answer, and explain, but, most of all, they listen intently and act promptly on customer suggestions and comments. Other organizations may hire professional moderators, rent a commercial facility complete with managerial viewing booths behind two-way mirrors, and even pay selected customers for their participation. In this case, the session is videotaped with the participants' knowledge and consent. The sponsoring organization receives a formal report that summarizes the results of the sessions and offers recommendations.

Whatever the particular arrangement, the purpose of focus groups is to encourage free-flowing discussion of issues relevant to an organization's customers and thus to the organization itself. Refreshments are usually served to create a relaxed atmosphere and it is useful to record the results at least on audiotape for subsequent replay and review. The moderator is responsible for keeping the discussion on topic and covering all important issues. Toward this end, it is helpful to draw up a moderator's guide or checklist of issues to address during the discussion.

Major benefits of focus groups are the spontaneity and synergy that arise when participants build on each other's comments. Also, the moderator has the unique opportunity to probe for details when an unexpected line of thinking emerges. The dynamics of group interaction make the serendipitous discovery of previously unknown concerns or opportunities a key benefit of focus group discussions. It is essential not to engage in headcounting or voting as this may belittle vital comments that individual participants offer.

Due to their versatility and speed, focus groups can be used for a variety of purposes in an organization's dialog with its customers. They can provide input into or feedback on the organization's actions and guide the design and/or interpretation of customer surveys. Focus group sessions are powerful research tools that must be used with care. One of their potential pitfalls is domination of the discussion by an outspoken participant.

SURVEYS

Organizations conduct large-scale customer studies with the help of questionnaires. Questionnaires are formal lists of questions with multiple answer choices from which respondents select one or more that fit their particular situations. These forms can be administered in person, over the phone, by fax, or through the mail to a sizable number of customers. In contrast to focus groups, which are qualitative research tools and thus can provide insights but no numbers, surveys are a means of quantitative research that can generate numerical measurements, such as frequency distributions.

Although surveys are popular tools, they should be used with caution. Organizations need to be concerned with their reliability and validity.

- *Reliability* refers to the accuracy with which the issues being investigated are measured. In other words, would another researcher, using the same survey instrument, come up with essentially the same results? Potential differences can arise from the respondent selection process, the response rate, and bias exerted by the interviewers, if any.

- *Validity* refers to whether the issues being investigated are appropriate. In other words, would another researcher, pursuing the same objectives, use the same questionnaire and ask the same respondents? A survey could well ask the wrong questions of the wrong people.

Questionnaire design is both an art and a science. Concerns relate, for instance, to the wording, sequencing, and number of the questions. All too often, questionnaires are written from the perspective and in the language of the researcher, not those of the customer. This may well lead to misunderstandings in the interpretation of questions or even meaningless results. Ideally, questionnaires should be designed with the help of customers and pretested with a small group of respondents before being rolled out on a large scale. Focus groups can be very helpful in this effort.

CRITICAL INCIDENT REPORTS

Customers are asked to report about recent experiences with an organization. In the customers' own words, these statements refer to incidents that matter to them. In this technique, customers recount recent interactions with employees of the organization and report how satisfied or dissatisfied they were with both the process and the outcome. Although such reports are somewhat difficult to quantify, they provide a treasure trove of information about moments of truth that affect their continued patronage. Where questionnaires present preconceived notions that may be of little concern to customers, critical incident reports reflect occurrences that continue to bother or delight customers. Their memories of these incidents not only have an impact on their own future behavior but are shared with others via word-of-mouth conversations and thus have a ripple effect on them.

Perhaps worst of all, the customers' feelings likely have not been shared with the organization on the customers' initiative. This deprives its management of invaluable insights on where to recognize excellence in action and how to improve its weaknesses. All too many organizations display an attitude that "no news is good news." This is a head-in-the-sand approach that says, "We are not receiving any complaints, therefore we must be dong well." Nothing could be further from the truth for mediocre organizations that continue to exist mainly for lack of effective competition. Most likely, the lack of complaints is not due to a lack of deficiencies but to a lack of an effective mechanism for reporting them.

ADVISORY PANELS

These groups of selected customer representatives advise organizations on a regular basis. Telephone companies, for instance, use such panels as sounding boards for new initiatives and services and to help them assess the nature and severity of complaints. The panels essentially act as spokespersons for the organization's customer base and assist in guiding its actions in a direction beneficial to both parties. Typically serving in a voluntary capacity, panel members tend to be vocal advocates of their constituencies, providing a vital and dynamic link to the marketplace.

ONE-ON-ONE CONVERSATIONS

These conversations involve invaluable personal contacts between individual employees and customers. A few organizations have developed this tool to the level of an art. Intuit, a California software developer and publisher, has designers interact with customers in its laboratory and visit them at home to observe them in action. Toyota had senior engineers travel with customers to help redesign vehicles for greater customer satisfaction. And, at the Ritz Carlton Hotel chain, which won the Baldrige Award for its world-class service, all employees record and report customer requests and comments on guest-preference forms. The data are entered into a database that is accessible to all of its properties worldwide. For its preferred customers, British Airways keeps a similar database available to all of its agents.

Continuous dialog with customers is an essential prerequisite for building and maintaining relationships with them that make them feel understood and appreciated. Excellence is impossible without closed-loop communications that facilitate the delivery of exceptional value to customers. At its core, creating customers for life means applying the golden rule that suggests treating others as we would like to be treated.

TOTAL COMMITMENT

While strategies and systems are important in giving direction and enabling action, customer delight depends most on an organization's employees. Careful selection, education, and empowerment of employees are at the heart of delivering excellence on a consistent, continuous basis.

Selecting the right employees is essential to their successful deployment in serving an organization's customers. While attitudes, skills, and knowledge can be taught, personality and character cannot. Help-wanted ads for McDonald's read "Smiles wanted." USAA, an insurance company in San Antonio, Texas, uses a nine-point "definition of a quality employee," an 11-point "personnel creed," and a multiple-step personnel acquisition process to create a top-notch work force. As an employer of choice, it receives an average of 37 applications for every open position and can thus be highly selective. This selectivity has paid off handsomely in an outstanding reputation among its loyal customers.

Disney shows prospective job applicants a video of what it's like to be inside the costume of one of its characters. As the sweat drips from a featured "cast member," about 20 percent of potential employees quietly leave the room, never to be seen again. As this example demonstrates, a growing number of organizations look for attitude, even more than aptitude, in potential recruits.

This fact is particularly evident in the selection procedure employed by Southwest Airlines. In a process more resembling a casting call for a movie than a typical job interview, candidates are marched into a large room and seated on its perimeter. Each is then asked to recount publicly the most embarrassing moment in his or her life. In the subsequent selection process, a team composed of human-resource professionals, flight attendants, and passengers assesses each candidate's character traits. First, and foremost, the company looks for a sense of humor in prospective employees as well as an exceptional level of energy.

Employee Education and Empowerment

Are exceptional performers born or made? The answer is probably a mixture of both. Hiring the right people is merely the beginning of a great performance. To live up to their potential, they must receive proper training and education. In fact, research clearly indicates that world-class organizations invest in the continuous development of their people through educational offerings tailored to their needs. Some have gone as far as to create formal "universities" or broad-based curricula of courses that are offered on an optional or mandatory basis.

But even the right employee selection and education go only so far in creating and sustaining excellent organizations. To be truly effective, they must be supported and guided by appropriate systems and strategies. And they must be empowered to take action on behalf of customers. *Empowerment* involves giving employees the right to act promptly on customer requests and do what it takes to please or even delight customers. Empowered employees do not have to obtain approval from superiors before responding to customer complaints or inquiries.

The Nordstrom department store chain encourages its employees to use their judgment in dealing with customers and to cross departments in serving their needs. At Federal Express, a front-line employee chartered a plane to fly equipment to Texas to help rescue a little girl who had fallen into a well. When the company's Chief Operating Officer was asked whether he had been consulted on this action, he replied that he hadn't and that the employee was well advised to use her judgment in the matter.

Empowering employees releases their judgment, initiative, and creativity in serving customer requirements. Because of their daily contact with customers, front-line employees know best how to please them. If they can act on this knowledge without being restricted by cumbersome rules and second-guessing superiors, they can serve as ambassadors in creating and maintaining customer goodwill. By acting promptly, they can even create customer delight and loyalty.

CUSTOMER-FRIENDLY PROCESSES

Achieving excellence for customers not only depends on continuous customer dialog and total employee commitment, it also requires customer-friendly processes. To be truly customer-friendly, an organization's processes must be characterized by teamwork, cycle time reduction, and the creation of customer value as symbolized by satisfaction guarantees.

Teamwork

The value an organization delivers to its customers is the result of an intricate process of cooperation between many individuals and units. A growing number of organizations are using the power of teamwork to reengineer their value-producing processes and improve customer service. They create self-directed teams that often cross traditional functional boundaries to eliminate non-value-added activities and speed up work flows.

A *self-directed team* is a cohesive group of broadly skilled employees who jointly own and manage a distinctive process. Such a team has no boss because its members share and rotate leadership responsibilities. The team hires, trains, and disciplines its own members who can and will substitute for and assist each other because they have a broad range of skills and are cross-trained to join forces seamlessly. The team sets its own goals after due consultation with its customers and inspects its own work to its own exacting standards. Its members plan, control, and improve their work processes continuously and coordinate their work carefully with other process teams.

Organizations that make the transition to self-directed teams are well on their way to sustained world-class performance. To make this approach work, organizations must delayer and flatten their traditional bureaucracies. Hierarchical vertical structures and their fiefdoms resist smooth horizontal coordination of customer-directed processes. Traditional managers who direct and control their subordinates must transform themselves into coaches—modern leaders who enable and support their associates.

At Johnsonville Foods in Johnsonville, Wisconsin, this powerful new approach has produced remarkable results. Former managers have redefined their roles as teachers and do not interfere with team decisions. Prospective members join a team on a probationary basis and have to prove themselves as genuine contributors before they are voted in. All pay increases are linked to the acquisition of new skills. And team members critically sample all products before shipping them to customers.

Guaranteed Satisfaction

Self-directed teams inevitably reduce cycle time dramatically, often from weeks to days, as they critically examine existing work processes and flows. At Titeflex, a maker of industrial hoses in Springfield, Massachusetts, order entry alone used to take weeks, followed by seemingly endless delays as the order wound its way through a disjointed manufacturing process. Although Titeflex hoses were prized for their superior quality, obtaining them in any kind of timely fashion was a nightmare for its customers. After redesigning its processes from scratch, the company can now enter most orders in minutes and can ship a rush order in hours. In fact, it can charge extra for its fast response in emergency situations.

In today's increasingly competitive marketplace, quick response to customer requests is a powerful weapon that frequently leads to higher prices and profits. So it is most worthwhile to take a clean-sheet approach to an organization's customer-directed processes and redesign them from the perspective of customer convenience and comfort. An organization that is easy to do business with and responds to customer needs in a speedy fashion is often rewarded with exceptional customer loyalty. The chief executive of a discount brokerage firm told a neighbor that his firm could execute the neighbor's trades at a lower cost than Charles Schwab. The neighbor replied that he was not interested because Charles Schwab provides him with superior service by confirming his trades immediately on the phone, offering electronic trading capability, and giving him toll-free access to his accounts and live information 24 hours a day, every day of the year.

An organization's ultimate commitment to customer-friendliness occurs in the form of satisfaction guarantees. The Embassy Suites hotel chain posts the following promise in all of its lobbies: "100% Satisfaction Guarantee. We guarantee high quality accommodations, clean, comfortable surroundings, and friendly and efficient service. If you're not completely satisfied, we don't expect you to pay."

A *satisfaction guarantee* is an enforceable promise that reduces a customer's perceived risk and ensures a desired outcome. It is a form of customer empowerment because it lets customers decide whether or not they are satisfied with the goods and/or services they received. A guarantee forces an organization to focus on customers and set clear performance standards. By encouraging customer feedback, it also helps identify and correct failure points in customer-directed processes.

5

THE POWER OF
CUSTOMER PASSION

Striving to create customers for life pays off handsomely for an organization in the form of customer loyalty and the resulting increase in profits. A Harvard Business School study substantiated the fact that customers become more profitable over time as the base profit from the relationship is augmented by increased purchases and/or higher balances, reduced operating costs, referrals of friends, and the ability to charge a price premium. The study determined that as a credit-card company reduces its customer defection rate from 20% to 10%, the length of its customer relationship doubles from five to ten years, and the net present value of the profit streams generated during this period more than doubles.

Carl Sewell has estimated the lifetime value of a customer of his Cadillac dealership in Dallas at $332,000. That's why he and his associates go out of their way to make customers feel welcome and appreciated. Salespeople introduce buyers to customer service personnel. Service advisors greet customers at the appointed time and provide a loaner car while the customer's vehicle is being serviced. Actual charges never exceed the detailed estimates and the mechanics place their business cards in the customers' vehicles upon completion to facilitate inquiries or comments.

Customers who feel an organization values them may formally affiliate with it as members. They may even enter into long-term agreements or strategic alliances with supplier organizations. And they may become friends who express their satisfaction and gratitude in a variety of ways.

CUSTOMERS AS MEMBERS

A growing number of organizations have realized that treating individual interactions with customers as discrete transactions is both inefficient and ineffective. It is inefficient because it requires the inconvenience of starting all over again from scratch with every single transaction. It is ineffective because it focuses narrowly on the here and now, but neglects the bigger, long-term picture.

Visits to hospital emergency rooms are examples of this kind of short-sighted perspective. Before a patient in acute distress even gets to see a caregiver, he or she must fill out extensive forms to ensure that appropriate insurance coverage exists. Meanwhile, precious time is lost in diagnosing and treating the current condition, and the patient's stress level increases needlessly. A much better approach would be to set up an account for a patient that records all relevant information in a data base and issue a card to the patient that could even be a smart card, carrying essential information on an embedded microchip. This way, diagnosis and treatment could commence immediately, and the patient would feed like a valued customer rather than a nuisance.

Building Lifetime Relationships

Enlightened organizations see great opportunities in transforming transactions into lifelong relationships and customers into members. While other card issuers have long referred to their customers as cardholders, American Express, Discover, and AT&T Universal Card think of them as members. In fact, American Express pioneered the concept of different classes of members with its green, gold, and platinum cards.

To establish stronger bonds with its passengers, American Airlines created its frequent flyer program in the early 1980s. The program became so popular with passengers that other airlines had to offer their own programs to remain competitive. The Admiral's Club, which operates special lounges in major airports and offers other benefits, invites business travelers to join.

Many nonprofit organizations have been able to leverage their relationships with their members for fundraising purposes with so-called affinity cards. Issued in conjunction with a major bank, such as MBNA, their use produces revenue flows to the sponsoring nonprofit organization every time the card is used, without costing the member an extra penny. This approach is known as cause-related marketing and was first used by American Express in support of the restoration of the Statue of Liberty.

Universities have long known the value of cultivating relationships with their alumni, especially for fundraising purposes. They have alumni relations offices and offer a variety of events and benefits to members of their alumni associations. Alumni are also a source of future students since they can recommend their alma mater and send their children.

CUSTOMERS AS PARTNERS

In today's fiercely competitive marketplace, no organization can be an island to itself. Rather, it needs to engage in strategic partnering to leverage its own capabilities and achieve its objectives. *Partnering* means joining forces with other organizations in long-term, mutually beneficial relationships. Increasingly, customer organizations question the way they have been dong business, and refocus their energies and resources on their core competencies. Consequently, they outsource noncore activities to external supplier organizations, building networks of interactive relationships in the process. Carefully choreographing their respective activities, they jointly produce value by orchestrating their contributions into a cohesive whole that exceeds the sum of the parts.

The Power of Partnering

Partnering requires a substantial mutual commitment between two or more organizations. To be successful, partnering must be based on trust, open communications, and a long-term perspective. Frequently, it also involves single sourcing, a strategy where a customer decides to place all of its business in a given product category with just one supplier, even though other sources are available. Such a concentration of purchases is typically accompanied by a multi-year agreement that assures both parties of the long-term nature of the relationship.

This may well translate into a helping hand. At Honda of America, Dave Nelson, Vice President of Purchasing, reports that he sends teams of engineers into supplier organizations to help them streamline their operations, reduce costs, and improve productivity. Ford and Xerox assist their suppliers in similar ways. Motorola and Toyota conduct training programs for supplier personnel to help them improve their efficiency and effectiveness.

It also makes sense to involve customers early in new product development to reduce risk and increase the likelihood of success. In the development of Boeing's new 777 airplane, a representative of United Airlines was a member of the development team. IBM and others invite customers to help them fine-tune new products prior to introduction. Marriott built model rooms for examination by guests before it finalized the design of its Courtyard motels. Innovation, in fact, may be driven by customers who bring their ideas or designs to preferred suppliers.

Partnering for Quality

Customers also partner with suppliers to achieve consistent quality of the inputs they receive from these external resources. The value an external customer ultimately receives depends substantially on the quality of the inputs obtained from suppliers. Any organization is only as good as its sources and, justifiably, is judged by the company it keeps. Accordingly, customers have every reason to select their suppliers carefully and proactively manage their relationships with them.

Quality is a moving target. Yesterday's quality is not good enough for tomorrow's demanding markets. Consequently, partnering for quality means joint efforts toward continuous improvement. Upon winning the Baldrige Award in 1988, Motorola announced that it would require all of its suppliers to apply for this prestigious quality prize. While that objective turned out to be overly ambitious, it is evident that just maintaining quality means falling back in the competitive race.

CUSTOMERS AS FRIENDS

It is the ultimate accolade for an organization and its employees when its customers become its friends. Some may counsel that business and friendship do not mix well, but any organization can benefit from having a "fan club."

Satisfied customers are an organization's most successful salespeople, because they do not stand to benefit financially from recommending the organization to others.

Recognizing Outstanding Supplier Performance

Friends say "thank you" to friends. Enthusiastic customers gratefully acknowledge outstanding service by sending letters of commendation to an organization's senior management, praising the exceptional performance of specific employees. These prized, unsolicited comments can make a great deal of difference in the self-esteem, job attitude, and career of an individual. Sometimes, such letters do not identify specific individuals, but rather, describe the total experience with an organization as a whole. Whatever the case, "fan mail" from customers is often posted on bulletin boards, published in newsletters, or shared with employees in meetings.

On a more formal level, some customer organizations give "Outstanding Supplier Awards" to selected supplier organizations who have performed exceptionally well. Such awards are usually presented in the form of plaques in official recognition ceremonies attended by teams from both sides. Subsequently, these coveted awards typically grace the lobbies of the honored supplier organizations.

Some customer organizations also certify selected supplier organizations. Typically using a stepladder approach, leading from newly approved supplier to world-class performance, the certification process tends to be an arduous one that only few suppliers can master. Certification means not only consistent zero defects, but also continuous improvement—a demanding standard, indeed. Ford and Xerox are among the companies that annually publish full-page advertisements in the *Wall Street Journal* to thank their certified suppliers for their contributions to the customer organizations' success.

Celebrating with Customers

Since friendship works both ways, it is just as appropriate for an organization to thank its customers for their patronage and support. Staples, an office supply company, tracks "member" purchases and periodically sends selected members savings coupons to be applied to their next purchases. Volkswagen dealers periodically mail service bonus certificates to preferred customers to reward their loyalty.

Some organizations designate "customer appreciation days," during which they offer special benefits to customers, ranging from free refreshments to special discounts. Others mail special presale invitations that offer loyal customers additional discounts.

The ultimate type of celebration of great relationships, however, are parties or reunions. Banks and telephone companies have been known to invite key customers to join the fun and have a good time at a special event, such as a celebrity golf or tennis tournament. Shouldice Hospital's annual reunion of former patients is usually oversubscribed. Universities also conduct periodic reunions, tailgate parties, and similar events to cultivate the relationships with their alumni.

6

EPILOG

For organizations that want to survive and prosper, creating customers for life is *the* strategic imperative. Substantial customer turnover is expensive and risky for any organization. It is said that it costs five times as much to gain a new customer than to hold on to an existing one. And it may not only be expensive, but quite difficult to replace departing customers. So it is essential to stem defections by satisfying, if not delighting, customers. It is also worthwhile to attempt to regain lost customers. After all, they may have found that the grass is not quite as green on the other side of the fence as they had originally thought. Surprisingly, they may be yearning to come back into the fold. Former customers of insurance agencies or stock brokerage houses may well have been disappointed by their new supplier and be ready to return.

It is worthwhile and exciting to turn one-time purchasers into lifelong friends by rendering exceptional service. Delighting customers is not only psychologically rewarding, but translates into growing profits. Customers for life are not swayed by competitive offers, but instead, bring more business to the organization. At the heart of every organization are two key assets: its employees and its customers. Customers for today may not be here tomorrow. Customers for life are the engine of survival and growth. They are every organization's reason for being and its future. Pleasing and, in fact, delighting them is not a luxury, but the key to sustained success.

BIBLIOGRAPHY

Bell, Chip R., and Ron Zemke. *Managing Knock Your Socks Off Service.* New York: AMACOM, 1992.

Carlzon, Jan. *Moments of Truth.* Cambridge, Mass.: Ballinger, 1987.

Hart, Christopher W.L. *Extraordinary Guarantees.* New York: AMACOM, 1993.

Reichheld, Frederick F. and W. Earl Sasser, Jr. "Zero Defections: Quality Comes to Services." *Harvard Business Review,* Sept.-Oct. 1990.

Sewell, Carl, and Paul B. Brown. *Customers for Life.* New York: Pocket Books, 1990.

Walther, George R. *Upside-Down Marketing.* New York: McGraw-Hill, 1994.

ABOUT THE AUTHOR

Eberhard E. Scheuing is professor of marketing, director of the Business Research Institute, and director of Executive Education at St. John's University in New York. Born and educated in Germany, he received his M.B.A. in management and his Ph.D. in marketing from the University of Munich.

The author of 23 books and more than 500 articles, Dr. Scheuing is the founder and president of the International Service Quality Association and a frequent seminar leader, conference speaker, and consultant.

Eberhard E. Scheuing, P.O. Box 516, Tivoli, NY 12583-2141.

PRAISE FOR THE MANAGEMENT MASTER SERIES

"A rare information resource.... Each book is a gem; each set of six books a basic library.... Handy guides for success in the '90s and the new millennium."

Otis Wolkins
Vice President Quality Services/Marketing
Administration, GTE

"Productivity Press has provided a real service in its *Management Master Series*. These little books fill the huge gap between the 'bites' of oversimplified information found in most business magazines and the full-length books that no one has enough time to read. They have chosen very important topics in quality and found well-known authors who are willing to hold themselves within the 'one plane trip's worth' length limitation. Every serious manager should have a few of these in their reading backlog to help keep up with today's new management challenges."

C. Jackson Grayson, Jr.
Chairman, American Productivity & Quality Center

"The *Management Master Series* takes the Cliffs Notes approach to management ideas, with each monograph a tight 50 pages of remarkably meaty concepts that are defined, dissected, and contextualized for easy digestion."

Industry Week

"A concise overview of the critical success factors for today's leaders."

Quality Digest

"A wonderful collection of practical advice for managers."

Edgar R. Fiedler
Vice President and Economic Counsellor,
The Conference Board

"A great resource tool for business, government, and education."

Dr. Dennis J. Murray
President, Marist College

PRODUCTIVITY PRESS, Dept. BK, PO Box 13390, Portland, OR 97213-0390
Telephone: 1-800-394-6868   Fax: 1-800-394-6286

THE MANAGEMENT MASTER SERIES

The Management Master Series offers business managers leading-edge information on the best contemporary management practices. Written by respected authorities, each short "briefcase book" addresses a specific topic in a concise, to-the-point presentation, using both text and illustrations. These are ideal books for busy managers who want to get the whole message quickly.

Set 1. Great Management Ideas

Management Alert: Don't Reform—Transform!
Michael J. Kami
Transform your corporation: adapt faster, be more productive, perform better.

Vision, Mission, Total Quality: Leadership Tools for Turbulent Times
William F. Christopher
Build your vision and mission to achieve world class goals.

The Power of Strategic Partnering
Eberhard E. Scheuing
Take advantage of the strengths in your customer-supplier chain.

New Performance Measures
Brian H. Maskell
Measure service, quality, and flexibility with methods that address your customers' needs.

Motivating Superior Performance
Saul W. Gellerman
Use these key factors—non-monetary as well as monetary—to improve employee performance.

Doing and Rewarding: Inside a High-Performance Organization
Carl G. Thor
Design systems to reward superior performance and encourage productivity.

PRODUCTIVITY PRESS, Dept. BK, PO Box 13390, Portland, OR 97213-0390
Telephone: 1-800-394-6868   Fax: 1-800-394-6286

Set 2. Total Quality

The 16-Point Strategy for Productivity and Total Quality
William F. Christopher/Carl G. Thor
Essential points you need to know to improve the performance of your organization.

The TQM Paradigm: Key Ideas That Make It Work
Derm Barrett
Get a firm grasp of the world-changing ideas beyond the Total Quality movement.

Process Management: A Systems Approach to Total Quality
Eugene H. Melan
Learn how a business process orientation will clarify and streamline your organization's capabilities.

Practical Benchmarking for Mutual Improvement
Carl G. Thor
Discover a down-to-earth approach to benchmarking and building useful partnerships for quality.

Mistake-Proofing: Designing Errors Out
Richard B. Chase and Douglas M. Stewart
Learn how to eliminate errors and defects at the source with inexpensive *poka-yoke* devices and staff creativity.

Communicating, Training, and Developing for
Quality Performance
Saul W. Gellerman
Gain quick expertise in communication and employee development basics.

PRODUCTIVITY PRESS, Dept. BK, PO Box 13390, Portland, OR 97213-0390
Telephone: 1-800-394-6868   Fax: 1-800-394-6286

Set 3. Customer Focus

Designing Products and Services That Customers Want
Robert King

Here are guidelines for designing customer-exciting products and services to meet the demands for continuous improvement and constant innovation to satisfy customers.

Creating Customers for Life
Eberhard E. Scheuing

Learn how to use quality function deployment to meet the demands for continuous improvement and constant innovation to satisfy customers.

Building Bridges to Customers
Gerald A. Michaelson

From the priceless value of a single customer to balancing priorities, Michaelson delivers a powerful guide for instituting a customer-based culture within any organization.

Delivering Customer Value: It's Everyone's Job
Karl Albrecht

This volume is dedicated to empowering people to deliver customer value and aligning a company's service systems.

Shared Expectations: Sustaining Customer Relationships
Wayne A. Little

How to create a process for sharing expectations and building lasting and profitable relationships with customers and suppliers that incorporates performance goals and measures.

Service Recovery: Fixing Broken Customers
Ron Zemke

Here are the guidelines for developing a customer-retaining service recovery system that can be a strategic asset in a company's total quality effort.

PRODUCTIVITY PRESS, Dept. BK, PO Box 13390, Portland, OR 97213-0390
Telephone: 1-800-394-6868   Fax: 1-800-394-6286

Set 4. Leadership (available November, 1995)

Leading the Way to Organization Renewal
Burt Nanus
How to build and steer a continually renewing and transforming organization by applying a vision to action strategy.

Checklist for Leaders
Gabriel Hevesi
Learn to focus day-to-day decisions and actions, leadership, communications, team building, planning, and efficiency.

Creating Leaders for Tomorrow
Karl Albrecht
How to mobilize all the intelligence of the organization to create value for customers.

Total Quality: A Framework for Leadership
D. Otis Wolkins
Consider the problems and opportunities in today's world of changing technology, global competition, and rising customer expectations in terms of the leadership role.

From Management to Leadership
Lawrence M. Miller
A visionary analysis of the qualities required of leaders in today's business: vision and values, enthusiasm for customers, teamwork, and problem-solving skills at all levels.

High Performance Leadership: Creating Value in a World of Change
Leonard R. Sayles
Examine the need for leadership involvement in work systems and operations technology to meet the increasing demands for short development cycles and technologically complex products and services.

PRODUCTIVITY PRESS, Dept. BK, PO Box 13390, Portland, OR 97213-0390
Telephone: 1-800-394-6868   Fax: 1-800-394-6286

ABOUT PRODUCTIVITY PRESS

Productivity Press exists to support the continuous improvement of American business and industry.

Since 1983, Productivity has published more than 100 books on the world's best manufacturing methods and management strategies. Many Productivity Press titles are direct source materials translated for the first time into English from industrial leaders around the world.

The impact of the Productivity publishing program on Western industry has been profound. Leading companies in virtually every industry sector use Productivity Press books for education and training. These books ride the cutting edge of today's business trends and include books on total quality management (TQM), corporate management, Just-In-Time manufacturing process improvements, total employee involvement (TEI), profit management, product design and development, total productive maintenance (TPM), and system dynamics.

To get a copy of the full-color catalog, call 800-394-6868 or fax 800-394-6286.

To view sample chapters and see the complete line of books, visit the Productivity Press online catalog on the Internet at *http://www.ppress.com/*

Productivity Press titles are distributed to the trade by National Book Network, 800-462-6420

TO ORDER: Write, phone, or fax Productivity Press, Dept. BK, P.O. Box 13390, Portland, OR 97213-0390, phone 800-394-6868, fax 800-394-6286. Send check or charge to your credit card (American Express, Visa, MasterCard accepted).

U.S. ORDERS: Add $5 shipping for first book, $2 each additional for UPS surface delivery. We offer attractive quantity discounts for bulk purchases of individual titles; call for more information.

ORDER BY E-MAIL: Order 24 hours a day from anywhere in the world. Use either address:
To order: *service@ppress.com*
To view online catalog on the Internet and/or to order:
  http://www.ppress.com/

INTERNATIONAL ORDERS: Write, phone, or fax for quote and indicate shipping method desired. For international callers, telephone number is 503-235-0600 and fax number is 503-235-0909. Prepayment in U.S. dollars must accompany your order (checks must be drawn on U.S. banks). When quote is returned with payment, your order will be shipped promptly by the method requested.

NOTE: Prices are in U.S. dollars and are subject to change without notice.

light

to follow is that variegated plants or plants with small, narrow leaves will need more light than all-green or large, wide-leaved plants. The reason for this variance is that there is more chlorophyll (the light-absorbing particles of photosynthesis) in plants with all-green or large, wide leaves than in plants with narrow or variegated leaves. Most variegated-leaved plants will produce more chlorophyll, thereby losing some of the variegation, when not given enough light.

Aspects of Light

Three aspects of light influence plant growth: intensity, duration, and quality. Light intensity is the amount of light that a plant receives on its leaf surfaces, which influences the manufacture of carbohydrates or the process of photosynthesis. Generally, the rate of photosynthesis is proportional to light intensity (up to a saturation point, which varies among species). Photosynthesis is not dependent on natural sunlight and can be initiated by any light source, provided the intensity and other light factors are adequate.

Duration of the lighting period is important to plants. All plants require a certain length and continuity of light. An excellent light intensity will be of no use to a plant if it is not of the proper duration.

Light quality (or color) is the third major factor in lighting for plants. All light sources emit certain light wavelengths, falling into the violet, indigo, blue, green, yellow, orange or red categories of the visible light spectrum. The chlorophyll pigments in plants absorb light mainly in the blue and red regions. The human eye is most sensitive in the green and yellow regions.

What is a Footcandle?

Candles

Light intensity is most commonly measured in footcandles. A footcandle is defined as the amount of light that one standard candle gives off one foot away.

A light meter will measure any source of light, either natural or artificial. Hold a sheet of plain white paper next to the top one-third of the plant, so the paper faces the light source. Measure available light intensity by aiming the meter at the paper. Relatively low-cost, pocket-size light meters that read directly in footcandles are available from electrical supply stores.

The simpler designations of low, medium, and high light are also used. Low light is defined as less than 75 footcandles, medium light as 75 to 200 footcandles, and high light as more than 200 footcandles. Many times, these designations are easier to understand.

Kinds of Light
Natural light is the least expensive and most beneficial source for plant growth.

If at all possible, foliage plants should be given light through windows or skylights. If this is not possible, artificial light can be substituted.

When natural light is not sufficient, several types of artificial light can be used: fluorescent, incandescent, high intensity discharge (HID) or combinations of these. Whichever types are used, it is important to consider not only light intensity, but also the photoperiod (length of time it is used). For any given minimum light intensity, lights will have to be on longer; at higher light intensity, 9 to 10 hours daily should be sufficient. The closer a plant is placed to a light source, the higher the light intensity it will receive.

Fluorescent Lighting

One of the most common sources of artificial light is fluorescent lamps. Cool white fluorescent lights contain relatively low amounts of red light and high amounts of blue light. Blue light tends to produce shorter, stockier and healthier-looking growth than red light alone.

Warm white tubes are high in red light and can cause plants to grow taller than when grown with cool white tubes. Cool white fluorescent lamps can be combined with incandescent lamps to produce light similar to that of the plant growth lamps. When this combination is desired, 20% of the wattage should be incandescent and 80% cool white fluorescent. The use of single-colored lamps is not recommended, because most colored lamps reduce the amount of available light and therefore, reduce growth. White lamps have balanced color spectrums and are the most efficient and best light sources for normal plant growth.

Light Bulb

Fluorescent Bulb

High Intensity Discharge (HID)

HID lamps emit light that is just as good for growing plants as that given off by fluorescent light. They are, however, more expensive, because they require a special transformer, as well as the expensive vapor bulb and reflector. The main advantage to HID is the long life of the lamp and greater efficiency of power consumption.

Incandescent Lighting

Incandescent lamps emit a high amount of energy as heat, rather than light, and are not as beneficial to plant growth. While the initial cost of installing incandescent lights is reasonable, they are expensive to use in the long run because of frequent replacement of the bulbs and the high cost of electricity. The heat emitted from incandescent bulbs can damage the leaves if they are too close to the lamp.

A Basic Guide to Understanding Light

Most people depend on the natural available light in their homes when growing and enjoying plants. Understanding what is meant by bright, indirect and low light is important. The following brief descriptions may help you better understand the light requirements of plants. Suggestions for lighting can serve as a guide for most parts of the United States and Canada. Some regions, particularly in the southern and western United States, will have very high light intensities. If you live in one of these areas, you will have to increase the distances from windows as necessary.

Bright Light

Sunny - Full sun for 5 hours in winter.
Bright Light - Up to 2 feet from east or west windows; up to 5 feet from south windows. (These light conditions may be too bright for the southern or western parts of the United States.)

Indirect or Bright Diffused Light

Indirect Light - Up to 4 feet from a north window; up to 8 feet from a south window; up to 5 feet from an east or west window. It is possible to place plants closer to a window if a screen or curtain is placed in front of the glass when the sun comes through.

Low Light

Shaded Light - Up to 6 feet from a north window; up to 8 feet from an east or west window; up to 10 feet from a south window.

Light must be adequate, able to cast a shadow. If it does not, the intensity is too low for survival of most plants.

light

Spots caused by excessive sun conditions.

Insufficient Light

When plants do not receive enough light, they grow slowly, require less water and need little or no fertilizer. Growth will stretch out and will look thin and spindly. Overwatering is often a problem because the plants will require less than normal amounts. Plants can be maintained in too-low light for awhile but eventually they will start to deteriorate. A plant given insufficient light may exhibit any or all of the following characteristics.

1. Growth will be stretched out, producing a tall, spindly-looking plant.
2. Leaves are smaller than normal; they may be curled or cupped.
3. Leaves may turn yellow and drop.
4. Normally variegated leaves lose their variegation.
5. Flowers are pale colored or absent.
6. Growth is slow, stunted, or absent. The plant may eventually die.

What can be done when light conditions are insufficient? Some suggestions are: leave lights on more hours each day; increase light intensity with supplemental lighting; move plants closer to the window; and avoid areas where light is obscured permanently or for long periods of time.

Excessive Light

Sun scorch is usually the result of excessive sunlight, enhanced by high temperatures. Rapid changes in light intensity can also cause problems. Sun scorch may occur when plants are placed outdoors in bright, sunny areas. It may occur if shade-loving plants are placed in areas too bright for them. Plants may also develop sun scorch problems if they are left in bright windows during summer. Sun-scorched plants will:

1. Wilt.
2. Develop bleached or transparent spots on leaves facing light.
3. Develop brown or scorched areas on leaves facing light.

If you wish to place your indoor plants outdoors, you should select a location which approximates indoor light levels to avoid sun scorch. A gradual process of moving plants outdoors will eliminate the possibility of sudden, damaging light changes. Outdoor light intensities are usually higher than those indoors.

water

Eighty to ninety percent of a plant is composed of water. All plant processes require water.

The environment, the plant itself, the type of growing medium and the type and size of pot are all factors relating to the frequency of watering.

Rainwater

Environment

The environment in which a plant lives has an important relationship to the watering process. It is a determining factor in the amount of water a plant uses. In a sunny location, plants lose more water than they do in shade. Warm temperatures and low relative humidity contribute to a greater water requirement.

The Plant Itself

Plants can be divided into three general categories according to their water requirements. Some plants require dry soil between each thorough watering. The length of this dry period may vary with each species of plant. Most plants prefer moderately moist soil. A few plants need soil that is very moist at all times. Proper watering may be difficult to achieve, but is certainly within every plant owner's capability.

Growing Medium

Soils will vary in their composition, and this can play an important role in determining the watering schedule. Soils containing large amounts of clay will hold more water, which can lead to overwatering. Plants in clay soils, therefore, need less frequent watering.

Soil can be loosened to permit better drainage and, therefore, more accurate watering, by the addition of coarse particles such as perlite, vermiculite and sand. Organic matter such as peat moss and humus can also be used to condition soil to drain adequately to meet the plant's needs. The primary consideration for any growing medium is that soil drains readily so that plant roots are not held in water, becoming vulnerable to root rot.

Type of Pot

The type of container used makes little difference if care is given when watering. Many people consider clay pots superior to other types. Actually, the principal reason for their greater success is that it is more difficult to over-water plants in clay pots since the pot allows some water to seep through and evaporate from the sides.

If you are careful when watering, any container material — plastic, Styrofoam™, metal, ceramic, or glass — can be used, as long as it is not toxic to the plant. Although pots with no drainage hole are less desirable, they are satisfactory if watered less frequently than those with drainage. Large pots do not need watering as often as small pots.

Methods of Watering

The easiest and probably most common approach is to apply enough water to the soil surface so that some water drains from the bottom of the pot. When watering from the top, do not allow water to remain on the leaves; this can encourage disease.

Types of Water

Water safe for human consumption is usually safe for plants. Softened water usually contains sodium, which can disperse the soil and break down soil structure, making it difficult for the roots to take up nutrients and oxygen.

Hard water contains calcium and magnesium, which help flocculate (build) soil structure so that nutrients can be held in the soil and taken up by the plant. Chlorinated drinking water can be used on plants with

Tap Water

no detrimental effects. The chlorinated water found in swimming pools, however, usually has too high of a concentration of chlorine. It is a good idea to use caution when placing plants in a pool area. Place them far enough away from the pool to prevent splashes from spotting the plants.

Fluoride and boron damage can be a problem in some parts of the United States. Fluoride damage causes necrosis (death of plant cells) of the leaves of certain plants. Superphosphate fertilizer and perlite are sources of fluoride that are sometimes found at damaging levels in growing media. A higher pH of the soil can decrease the toxicity of fluoride. In some parts of the United States, boron toxicity can also be a problem.

Pool Water

When to Water

Of the many methods used to determine watering schedules, the most successful for most plant owners is to feel the soil. Checking the soil surface daily gives you some idea of the amount of water used by the plant.

Plants that need their soil to dry out between thorough waterings shouldn't be watered until the top layer of soil feels dry. Plants that need to be kept moderately moist can be watered when the soil first feels dry to the touch. Plants requiring constantly moist soil should never be allowed to dry out. The surface of the soil should always be moist to the touch.

Touch alone is not a foolproof method of checking. Soil in large pots could be dry on top and still be moist at the bottom or even at the center of the soil mass. Pots of any size could be dry at the bottom and moist on top because of sprinkling, instead of thorough watering.

Two alternatives to the "feel" method help judge the need for water. One is the "cake testing" method in which any thin probe is inserted into the soil mass. If "crumbs" of soil cling to the sides of the probe as it is pulled out, moisture is present. If the tester comes out clean, it is an indication of dry soil.

Another test is the weight method. After a thorough watering (water draining out of the bottom), the pot will be heavy. Judged against this weight, you can pick up a pot and determine if it seems a little lighter or considerably lighter. The lighter the pot, the drier the soil, and the greater the need for rewatering.

Leaching

This technique could also be called "what to do if you overfertilize." It is used to wash excess fertilizer salts out of the soil. To leach: water the plant from the top repeatedly until the drainage water is quite clear as it comes out of the drainage hole. When soluble salts from fertilizers build up in the soil, they cause water to flow out of the roots and into the soil, the reverse of the normal water uptake process. If watering is done properly, leaching should not be needed.

Minerals

Under Watering

To avoid under watering, water more thoroughly and more often.

This is most damaging to plants when they are in a drafty location or in low humidity areas, since more water is lost through the leaves in these situations. Under watering is caused by several factors. Frequently the problem is sparse and shallow watering, which does not allow roots to develop and grow deeply; therefore, the plant cannot tolerate dry spells. Avoid frequent shallow watering or watering from the bottom because this can cause fine, white-crusted salts to form on the soil surface. Watering on a schedule, rather than according to a plant's needs, can also be a problem. Generally, plants grow faster in high light conditions and require more water than in other conditions.

The following symptoms indicate that plants have been under watered:

1. The entire plant wilts; leaves drop and become curled or cupped.
2. The edges and tips of the leaves turn brown. Entire leaves eventually turn brown and drop.
3. There is a general drop of green leaves.
4. Roots are brown and dry.

Some plants will recover from wilt, while others won't. Know the water requirements of each plant.

Lack of water will often accentuate symptoms of overfertilization. Check how often and how much you fertilize; too little fertilizer is better than too much.

Overwatering

Overwatering is the most common mistake. Plants require air, as well as water, for healthy roots.

The soil in containers provides only a limited amount of space for air and water. If water fills all of these spaces, then the resulting oxygen deficiency can severely damage or kill roots. A few thorough waterings are better than daily doses for established plants. The goal should be well-drained soil that is evenly moist. Plants should not stand in water.

Lower foliage loss due to hot conditions without water.

Overwatering is often the result of underestimating the water-holding capacity of the container. Often, the fact that plants are in low light areas where they require less water is ignored.

These symptoms indicate plants have been overwatered:

1. **The whole plant wilts.**
2. **The lower leaves turn yellow and drop; others get brown and black spots.**
3. **The whole plant is stunted and fails to grow.**
4. **Stems and roots become brown, mushy and decayed.**

If a plant has been overwatered, place it in a warm place to allow it to dry out faster. Water less frequently. Don't water at all if the soil is moist and the plant is wilting. It is important to note weather, seasons and growth of the plant. For example, cloudy winter months provide less light, so plants grow less and need less water.

Overwatering can produce yellowed leaves.

temperature

Tolerance

Drafts, humidity and excessive temperature changes are environmental factors that can affect the well-being of plants.

Most foliage plants have been chosen over the years for their ability to withstand normal home temperatures of 65-75°F. Many can tolerate an even wider range of temperatures. Freezing temperatures will kill foliage plants, however, and temperatures over 85°F for long periods of time will result in poor growth. When light conditions are less than optimum, temperatures must also be reduced to prevent rapid drying out of the soil, poor plant growth and possible plant loss.

While plants can tolerate wide ranges in temperatures, changes must be gradual. Nothing affects a plant so adversely as a sudden change. Large plants usually drop more leaves following environmental changes, simply because they have more leaves than small plants.

Air Drafts — Warm & Cold

Warm drafts, such as those from a heat register, can cause damaging water loss. Wilting of the entire plant can occur, as can dropping of lower green leaves, while leaf tips and margins turn brown. Place plants in a location where they won't be subjected to direct hot air from heating ducts or other heating sources. Redirect air away from the plant if possible.

Cold drafts will wilt and crumple plant areas subjected to the cold. Some leaves and shoots may take on an olive green, water-soaked appearance. Air conditioning does not harm plants unless they are in the direct flow of the airstream. Place plants in a location where they will be out of cold drafts, and avoid placing plants on drafty windowsills during the winter. Temperatures of 40-45°F or below may cause leaf drop or chill damage. If you live in a cold winter climate and buy a plant in the winter, be sure it is wrapped when you take it home to protect it from the cold.

Hot conditions dry out soil.

Brown tips caused by low humidity.

Relative Humidity

Many homes have environments with low relative humidity, at least lower than indoor plants require to grow well. Heating, especially forced-air heat, and air conditioning tend to lower the relative humidity.

One method of raising the relative humidity in the home is to purchase a humidifier. Many humidifiers will raise the humidity to 30% and sometimes up to 50%. Another way of increasing humidity is through the use of a pebble tray or humidity tray. Fill a saucer at least as wide as the plant with pebbles. Place water so that it comes just below the top of the pebbles. Place the pot containing the plant on the pebbles. As water evaporates, add more water to the pebble tray. The evaporation of water from the pebbles will raise the relative humidity around the plant.

Plants raise the relative humidity around themselves through transpiration. Therefore, a third way of increasing humidity is to take advantage of this fact by grouping plants together. Plants that require the highest relative humidity should be placed in the center of this grouping.

Another method often suggested to increase humidity is "misting." Misting is adding fine drops of water to the air around the plant. This method is effective only if the plant is misted every 15 minutes and the person doing the misting does not move. If the person misting the plant walks away, the humidity that was provided will likely follow in the draft that's created. Plant owners usually mist plants until they are water-soaked, and this can lead to disease and overwatering problems.

Signs that the relative humidity is too low include:

1. Slowed plant growth.
2. More frequent watering required.
3. Brown leaf tips and edges.
4. Reduced flowering.

High humidity, usually not a common problem, can provide an ideal environment for leaf diseases. Water drops left on the leaves of some plants may also cause wet, blackened areas.

Temperature Extremes

Excessively warm temperatures are often related to light. Leaves may wilt, yellow and fall off. When transporting plants, don't leave them in a hot car. Avoid tops of radiators, television sets, fireplaces (in use) or the tops of other heated surfaces.

Excessively cold temperatures will cause leaves to wilt and curl. They will become discolored or entirely brown and then drop off. Protect plants from cold drafts and

Frost can destroy some plants.

cold injury. When transporting plants, protect them with coverings and don't leave them in the car for an extended period of time.

fertilizer

What Does it Do?

Plants require a number of nutrients in order to grow properly.

Fertilizers are available in tablets, powders, liquids, slow-release forms and foliage sprays in every quantity and color imaginable. So it is no wonder that fertilizers and fertilization programs are so confusing to many consumers.

As a general rule, fertilization should become part of the maintenance program whenever plants are in an interior environment for six months or longer. Fertilizer applications should be geared to the amount of growth desired or the possibility of growth. Generally, the more plants grow and new foliage develops, the more fertilizer is needed. But sometimes it may be desirable to simply maintain the existing foliage of indoor plants and not encourage any new growth. Under low light conditions, new growth tends to have wide, thin leaves that would differ considerably from the original foliage produced under higher light conditions.

Each plant species varies somewhat in its response to a nutrient deficiency and may not show the classic symptoms. Also, when one nutrient is lacking, it may be that others are lacking as well, and the symptoms observed may actually result from multiple causes.

In most cases, it is desirable to have a soil test or foliage analysis conducted to determine a particular deficiency. These tests are available through private laboratories or your state agricultural university.

Macronutrients

Macronutrients are nutrients that are required in large quantities.

Nitrogen: Nitrogen is the most important of the soil nutrients. Plants that do not have an adequate source of nitrogen will exhibit chlorotic (yellowish) new growth and older leaves will turn yellow and drop. Overall, growth is stunted. An over-application of nitrogen will result in an excess of vegetative growth and few flowers.

Phosphorus: Phosphorus is important to energy transformations in the plant, especially those involving flowering, root development, and resistance to certain

Fertilizer and seedling

diseases. Plants with a phosphorus deficiency exhibit spindly growth and a purplish color on older foliage.

The use of superphosphate as a fertilizer (usually mixed into soil before use) has been shown to be a source of fluoride. Fluoride toxicity has resulted in burned tips and brown edges on leaves of dracaena, chlorophytum and cordyline.

Potassium: Potassium is necessary for the development of chlorophyll (the green pigment of plants). It also plays an active role in encouraging the development of a good root system and increasing resistance to certain diseases. The plant's older leaves lose potassium to the newer ones, resulting in a potassium deficiency that causes the leaf margins of these older leaves to gradually lose their green color (become chlorotic). These leaves may also turn brown.

Calcium: Calcium helps the physical structure of soils, modifies chemical reactions in the soil and makes other nutrients more easily available to plants. Signs of calcium deficiency occur at the growing tips of plants. The margins of leaves do not develop properly and give a crinkled appearance. Terminal growth is stunted and abnormal. Stunted, stubby roots may develop.

Magnesium: Magnesium is similar to calcium in its effects on soil structure and pH. Mature leaves develop interveinal chlorosis (veins are green, and areas between are yellowish) when magnesium is deficient. Magnesium will translocate, so the same symptoms may be exhibited on young leaves.

Sulfur: Sulfur is important to certain enzymatic reactions and may be used to lower the soil pH. Plants deficient in sulfur develop chlorosis over the whole plant and may develop a beige cast. Sulfur deficiency is rare.

Micronutrients

Micronutrients are used in small quantities.

Symptoms of micronutrient deficiencies occur only at the tip of the plant on newer leaves.

Boron: Buds and new leaves that develop a light green coloration exhibit a classic boron deficiency. The terminal bud or tip may also die.

Copper: Young leaves will exhibit a wilted appearance, develop a cupped formation and eventually show marginal browning. Some interveinal chlorosis may develop on young leaves.

Iron: New leaves exhibit interveinal chlorosis, which may later become completely yellow or even white.

Manganese: Interveinal chlorosis develops as with iron except with a definite pattern, more striped or checkered in appearance. Gray or brown spots may develop in the yellowish areas.

Forms of Fertilizer

Fertilizers have been categorized into five forms: liquid, soluble crystals, soluble tablets, slow-release and all-organic.

1. Liquid fertilizers are packaged as a solution. A specific quantity of fertilizer is mixed with a certain amount of water and then applied to plants.

2. Soluble crystals are packaged as dry salts, which will completely dissolve when added to water.

3. Soluble tablets are tablets formed from a pre-measured amount of fertilizer. The tablets dissolve completely when added to water.

4. Slow-release fertilizers release nutrients over a relatively long period of time. Formulations commonly used on foliage plants have a 3 to 4 month release time.

5. All-organic fertilizers release low amounts of nutrients over a long period of time.

Fertilizers are formulated with the three most important macronutrients as the primary constituents: nitrogen, phosphorus, and potassium. The nutrients are always listed in this order. As an example, a 10-10-10 fertilizer has 10% nitrogen, 10% phosphorus, and 10% potassium. An acceptable ratio of nutrients for foliage plants would be 1-1-1, 2-1-1, 2-1-2, 3-2-2, or 3-1-2. A 10-10-10 fertilizer would have a ratio of 1-1-1.

Fertilizer Rates

Generally, fertilizer works best when applied according to manufacturers' directions. Fertilize at regular recommended intervals so it is available to the plant when it is actively growing. For most plants, this will be during the spring and summer months, when light levels are high and the air temperature is warm.

Plants that have been recently placed into an interior environment should not be fertilized for at least three months. If plants are received directly from a production area, it may be necessary for the soil to be leached to remove high levels of fertilizer. The high levels of fertilizer used in production may be detrimental to the plant when it's placed in an interior environment.

growing medium
How Important Is It?

Water and nutrients provide a healthy balance.

The growing medium is an important and too-often neglected factor in plant success. Medium condition and characteristics largely determine root health. The medium should not only provide water and nutrients necessary for healthy balance, but also a good physical and biological environment for the roots. Poor aeration and drainage, incorrect pH, or a soluble salt accumulation are the most common soil conditions that can stress the root system.

Components of a Good Planting Medium

As a general rule, a suitable medium should be uniform and disease- and pest-free. Ideally, it should consist of 50% solid particles, 25% water space and 25% air space. A variety of materials are available for preparing a growing medium. Usually two or three of these ingredients are mixed together to prepare the medium.

Soil: The best soil is loam, a soil that is a combination of sand, silt and clay. Loam soil does not exhibit the dominant physical characteristics of any of the three

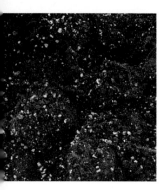

Rich soil helps plants.

groups. Sandy loams or silt loams are best for use in containers, as they have a balance of pore sizes to facilitate aeration and drainage.

Organic Material: Organic material is often added to the soil to loosen it, provide for drainage of water and entry of air, and to improve water retention. It is desirable for the organic material to be coarse-textured and decay resistant. One good organic material is sphagnum moss. Sphagnum moss has a slightly acid pH and excellent water-holding capacity. Other good sources of organic material include wood products, such as sawdust and bark. In certain regions of the country, products such as peanut hulls, rice hulls or ground corncobs are available.

Coarse Aggregates: Coarse aggregates are added to the medium to improve aeration and drainage. Sand is the least expensive and heaviest of the materials available, but it may be contaminated with pathogens and must be pasteurized.

Perlite: Perlite is expanded volcanic rock that is lightweight but has little ability to hold nutrients. It should be used in limited quantities because of the high fluorine content.

Vermiculite: This is an expanded micaceous mineral. It is available in many sizes and is able to hold nutrients and moisture.

When natural soil is used as part of a growing mix, standardization of the medium is difficult. For this reason, using a soilless mix may be desirable. Many types of soilless media are available on the market. Each should be evaluated, as they are mixed with different components, to determine the best one for the situation.

How Do Soil Conditions Relate to Plant Health?

Root health is frequently overlooked when maintaining plants in the home or interior plantscapes. Leaf drop, yellowing, stunting, and browning are just a few of the symptoms associated with plant root stress. If these symptoms are present, an inspection of the root-soil environment may prove helpful. Removing the plant from the container will allow a more thorough examination of the roots.

When examining the root system, look for definite characteristics of a healthy root system. White roots with good branching characteristics will be distributed throughout the soil. Be especially aware of the color and number of root tips. When the plant cannot be removed from the container, a soil probe that removes a core of soil and roots can be used.

Aeration: Good soil aeration ensures a proper supply of oxygen to, and removal of carbon dioxide from, the root zone. Soil pores must remain open and air-filled following irrigation for good aeration. When aeration is restricted there is a reduction of available soil oxygen and a possible increase in toxic soil gases, creating an unhealthy situation for the root system. This increases the probability of soil disease organisms becoming established.

Soil mixes with high quantities of clay, peat or fine bark have good water-holding properties. However, these fine-textured components can clog air space, creating poor drainage and aeration. Mixes high in properly milled bark, sand, perlite or vermiculite have good aeration and drainage but a low water-holding capacity. Plants in these mixes may dry more rapidly and must be watered more frequently. For best results, use a medium with a combination of components to provide good drainage and aeration in addition to increased water-holding capacity.

pH: Soil pH influences plant health by its effect on nutrient availability. At a pH of 7.0, the soil is neutral. Above 7.0, the soil is alkaline; below 7.0, it is acid. Nutrient deficiencies can occur when availability decreases due to an unfavorable pH. An unfavorable pH could be the result of a pH being either too high or too low. The best pH range to ensure availability of all nutrients to most plants is 6.2 to 6.8.

Soluble Salts: Salt concentration in the soil and in the root cells largely determines the amount of water that flows between the two. When soluble salts build up in the soil, water no longer moves into the roots. As a result, the plant wilts, overall growth slows, and the roots die back from the tips. Leaves may brown and die along their margins. Eventually nutrient deficiency symptoms are seen due to the injured root system.

Some soluble salts must be present for adequate nutrition, but the level must not be so high as to cause damage. Excessive salts in the soil can be due to overfertilization, poor water quality, or improper watering practices.

Proper watering is critical for a healthy plant. Small amounts of water applied frequently can leave dry areas or wet and dry borders in the soil mix, which can accumulate high salts. To prevent this, apply enough water so that some drains out of the container. The result will be an even distribution of water and fertilizer throughout the soil mass. Remove any excess drainage water so it is not reabsorbed by the soil. Soluble salts may quickly accumulate to damaging levels if this is not done.

repotting plants

How to Repot

Plants can be grouped together in one container as a dish garden or combination pot. The plants should have compatible cultural requirements and should not be packed too tightly.

Different pot sizes are beneficial.

Repotting is required if the plant has been potbound or if one or more plants are to be placed in decorative containers.

Guidelines for repotting:

1. Moisten the soil so the root ball will slip out easily.
2. Turn the pot over and tap the edge gently until the root ball slides out.
3. If roots are twisted and clinging tightly together, remove some of the "shoulder" of soil and untangle the outermost roots on the bottom of the ball. Be careful not to crumble root ball.
4. Repot into a clean pot slightly larger than the old one (usually 1 or 2 inches larger). Do not pot a small plant in a very large container hoping the plant will "grow into" its new home. This situation is conducive to overwatering because it will be based on pot size, not plant size.

5. Place pieces of clean, broken clay pot or gravel in the bottom of the containers with drainage holes.

6. Put a layer of soil over this drainage material.

7. Place root ball into pot and fill sides with soil, pressing in gently around root ball.

8. Do not put soil on top of root ball except to replace removed "shoulders." Raise level of soil by adding soil to the bottom only. Allow at least 1/2 inch below the rim of the pot for watering, so ample water may be applied without overflowing.

9. Water thoroughly, then allow the pot to drain, if drainage holes are present.

Slide root ball out.

Many decorative containers, unfortunately, have no drainage hole, making it difficult to grow plants in them. These plants soon lose their original purpose: decoration. For this reason, it is a good idea, especially with larger plants, to use the technique called double potting. To double-pot: Put gravel in the bottom of the decorative container. Set the plant, in its original clay or plastic pot, inside the decorative one. Fill the sides between the two pots with sphagnum peat moss. This method allows for good drainage, reduces the frequency of watering and still makes an attractive planter.

A similar method can be used with a decorative basket. A heavy, good quality polyethylene bag, such as a trash bag, can be used as a liner for any basket. A Styrofoam™ block can be put in the bottom of the basket to prevent the plant from standing in excess drainage water. Set the plant in the basket. Roll down any extra length of plastic liner (bag) and tuck it around the inside of the basket. Cover with Spanish moss for a finished, professional look.

Tap pot until soil falls out.

Propagating Your Plants

Plants are propagated using one of two principles of reproduction, asexual or sexual. Asexual propagation includes the use of cuttings, divisions, runners and stolons, and air layering. New plants produced by asexual reproduction are identical to each other and usually identical to the parent plant as well. This ability of a plant to form new plants from pieces of its stems, leaves and roots is largely dependent on the layer of tissue just below the outside surface. This layer will form a protective callus tissue when cut or removed from the parent plant. It is from this callus that the new roots and shoots will develop.

Seedlings

The second principle of plant propagation, sexual, involves the use of seeds. Sexual propagation is often less expensive than asexual and is easily accomplished. Packaged seed is usually ready for planting. Just follow the instructions on the package for planting procedures.

Good environmental conditions, proper sanitation for disease control, and suitable equipment are basic to plant propagation. An understanding of plant propagation methods is also critical to success. Common propagation methods use stem cuttings, leaf cuttings, leaf-bud cuttings, spores, seeds, grafting, runners and stolons, divisions and air layering.

Stem Cuttings: One of the most common methods of propagating plants in the home is easy to do, and usually produces fast results. Pruning an old plant to acquire cuttings also reconditions the plant by encouraging new branching.

Leaf-Bud Cuttings: A leaf-bud cutting consists of a leaf, a bud and a small section of stem and is used primarily for propagating costly, rare plants. This method requires more time for developing new growth.

Seeds come in many forms.

Leaf Cuttings: Leaf cuttings use all or part of the leaf blade and stem. Three types of leaf cuttings are: entire leaf blade and its stem, entire leaf blade with cut veins, and a section of leaf blade. The new roots and shoots are formed at the leaf base, from the veins or along the stem. The original leaf seldom becomes part of the new plant. It is usually discarded when the new plants are transplanted.

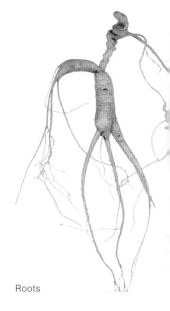

Roots

Spores: Ferns do not flower, and therefore cannot produce seed. They reproduce by microscopic organs called spores, which appear on the back of fronds (fern leaves). Sometimes mistaken for insects or disease, spores actually are easily identified by their orderly arrangement on the frond. The spores from a single frond can produce many new ferns, but the reproductive process may take several months.

Seeds: Propagation by seed can be used for many houseplants and is an inexpensive method of getting large numbers of new plants. It is necessary to buy good quality seeds if you expect good germination and healthy, strong plants that are true to type.

Grafting: Grafting is the union of two compatible plants so they will grow as one. It is done for many reasons, including earlier flowering, better root systems, and the development of plants that are more decorative. It is essential that only healthy plants be chosen for grafting.

Runners and Stolons: Some plants produce plantlets on runners (stems that develop from the crown of a plant) or stolons (stems that grow horizontally and produce roots when they touch a growing medium). This method has the advantage of producing new plants without cutting into the old plant. Plantlets can be detached from the old plant and placed in rooting medium.

Division: Propagation by division is used to separate plants with multiple crowns. Crowns are part of the plant at the ground surface where new shoots arise. They can split apart and the divisions can be grown separately.

Air Layering: This method involves rooting the stem of a plant without completely detaching it from the old root system. The advantage over cuttings is that while part of the stem forms roots, the other part can transport water to the leaves. Large plants can often be grown faster by air layering, because cuttings of equal size would lose too much water through their leaves to survive.

propagation

Basic steps for propagation:

1. Choose a container with good drainage.
2. Use a well-drained, sterilized planting medium.
3. Water the medium thoroughly and allow it to drain.
4. Take a cutting of proper size.
5. Use a hormone on the cutting (optional).
6. Insert the cutting into the planting medium.
7. Cover the container and cutting medium with clear plastic or glass.
8. Provide the proper environmental conditions: generally, low light, high humidity and warm temperatures.
9. Wait until the cutting has rooted before transplanting.
10. After transplanting, protect young plants from extremes in environment.

For more information on propagating plants, consult your library for reference books, and your local plant professionals for assistance. The Internet can also be a good source of information.

notes and sources:

African Violet

Saintpaulia ionantha
(saynt-PALL-ee-ah eye-oh-NAN-thah)

Light: Indirect or bright, diffused light.

Water: Moderately moist soil. Water thoroughly when just the soil surface is dry to the touch. Do not allow plants to stand in water.

Temperature: Warm – 70-75°F days and 65-70°F nights.

African Violet

African violets are available in a variety of colors including shades of white, red, blue, purple, violet and bicolors. African violets will flower continuously in good natural light conditions or with 14-16 hours of artificial light per day. Very high light can cause yellow leaves, but inadequate light will discourage flowering. Avoid splashing cold water on leaves, as this can cause yellow spots. Remove wilted flowers and leaves to discourage rot. Watch for cyclamen mites, mealybugs and aphids. Remove dying leaves to avoid gray mold and crown rot.

Aloe, Medicinal

Aloe barbadensis   *Also known as Aloe Vera*
(AL-oh-ee bar-ba-DEN-sis)

Light: Bright light, but can be maintained for many weeks in lower light.

Water: Moderately moist soil. Water thoroughly when just the soil surface is dry to the touch. Do not allow plants to stand in water.

Temperature: Moderate/Warm – 65-75°F days and 60-70°F nights.

Medicinal aloe is easy to grow. It is tolerant of various growing conditions as long as it has good drainage. The thick sap of the aloe vera hastens healing when applied to cuts and burns. Aloe should be kept drier during the fall and winter. Overwatering can be a problem, so be sure to provide good drainage. Watch for scale and mealybugs.

Medicinal Aloe

Amaryllis

Hippeastrum hybrid
(hip-ee-AS-trum)

Light: Indirect or bright, diffused light.

Water: Moderately moist soil. Water thoroughly when just the soil surface is dry to the touch. Do not allow plants to stand in water.

Temperature: Cool/Moderate – 60-70°F days and 55-65°F nights.

Amaryllis bulbs are usually available from December through April, in a variety of colors including shades of red, orange, white and bicolors. The impressive amaryllis stalk grows quickly from its bulb, followed by long, strap-like leaves. Dramatic blooms can be up to 6 inches across. Bright light promotes best growth. The stem may need staking to support the flowers. Each bloom lasts 3-4 days, the entire flowering period lasting 1-2 weeks.

Reflowering: After flowering, cut off the flowering stalk, place in bright light and continue care to let the foliage mature. In the fall, withhold water and allow the bulb 2 months of dormancy in a cool place (not freezing). You may continue to water, but flowering will not be as predictable. If necessary, repot with 1/3 of the bulb above the soil surface and about an inch of soil between the bulb and the edge of the pot. In a bright location, water sparingly until the flower stalk emerges, then water daily. Reflowering will occur in about 8 weeks.

Amaryllis

Anthurium

Anthurium
(an-THUR-ee-um)

Light: Bright light in winter and indirect light in summer.

Water: Moderately moist soil. Water thoroughly when just the soil surface is dry to the touch. Do not allow plants to stand in water.

Anthurium

Temperature: Moderate – 65-75°F days and 60-65°F nights.

Anthurium is easy to grow, but requires a little special attention. Its attractive dark green foliage and colorful flowers make it a nice complement to any setting. Anthurium requires high humidity to flower but holds its blooms well in any interior environment.

ARALIA PLANTS
False Aralia

Dizygotheca elegantissima
(dih-zih-GOTH-ih-cah el-eh-gan-TISS-ih-mah)

Light: Indirect or bright, diffused light.

Water: Moderately moist soil. Water thoroughly when just the soil surface is dry to the touch. Do not allow plants to stand in water.

Temperature: Warm – 70-75°F days and 65-70°F nights.

The unusual leaves grow broader as the plant matures. Red spider mites, scale and mealybugs can be problems, but the most common problem is dropping of the lower leaves. This is sometimes in response to overwatering, but low light, low humidity, dry soil, drafts and soluble chemicals in the soil may also be the cause.

False Aralia

Japanese Aralia

Fatsia japonica
(FAT-see-uh juh-PON-ih-kah)

Light: Indirect or bright, diffused light.

Water: Moderately moist soil. Water thoroughly when just the soil surface is dry to the touch. Do not allow plants to stand in water.

Temperature: Cool – 60-65°F days and 55-60°F nights.

The broad, lobed leaves of the Japanese aralia make a striking, bushy display. If you remove the flowers, the leaves will grow even larger, with the plant potentially reaching over 4 feet. Avoid very high light, since this can yellow the leaves. If your location is not as cool as preferred, it helps to increase the humidity. Watch for red spider mites and whiteflies.

Japanese Aralia

Ming Aralia

Ming Aralia

Polyscias fruticosa 'Elegans'
(pol-ISS-ee-us fru-ti-KOH-sa)

Light: Bright light, but can be maintained for many weeks in lower light.

Water: Moderately moist soil. Water thoroughly when just the soil surface is dry to the touch. Do not allow plants to stand in water.

Temperature: Warm – 70-75°F days and 65-70°F nights.

The juvenile and mature leaf shapes are different from each other, providing further interest as the plant grows. Leaf drop is the most common problem, resulting from change in environment, low light, chilling and improper watering. Ming aralias prefer high humidity. Watch for red spider mites.

Azalea

Azalea

Rhododendron or Indicum Hybrids
(row-doe-DEN-dron IN-di-kum)

Light: Indirect or bright, diffused light.

Water: Moderately moist soil. Water thoroughly when just the soil surface is dry to the touch. Do not allow plants to completely dry out or stand in water.

Temperature: Cool – 60-65°F days and 55-60°F nights.

Azalea are available in many flower forms and colors including white, pink, salmon, red, purple and variegated. Indoor varieties are available throughout the year and may flower from 2-8 weeks depending on quality of plant. To extend the flowering period, place the plant in a cool location (50-69°F) at night. Protect azalea from full sunlight, which may burn the flowers. Pinch off any young, green shoots that may extend beyond the flowers. Azalea need acid soil or their leaves may yellow. Watch for scale, leaf miners and whiteflies. Some varieties may be planted outdoors in partial sun.

Plant in a sheltered location with protection from wind, sun and winter conditions.

Reflowering: Azalea require a complicated set of treatments to reflower. The easiest way to get a flowering azalea for the next year is to buy one and let the growers worry about meeting all necessary treatments.

Rieger Begonia
Begonia x hiemalis
(beg-OWN-ya hie-MAL-is)

Rieger Begonia

Light: Bright light.

Water: Moderately moist soil. Water thoroughly when just the soil surface is dry to the touch. Do not allow plants to stand in water.

Temperature: Moderate – 65-70°F days and 60-65°F nights.

Rieger begonias are popular in spring but are available throughout the year in many striking colors including orange, yellow, white, cream and peach. This showy plant has large flowers up to 2 inches across and will bloom continuously under proper conditions. Excellent in summer for pots or hanging baskets in shady locations outdoors. Cut back stems 3 or 4 times during the year to maintain shape. Rieger begonias do not like high night temperatures (over 70°F), which can cause flower drop. High humidity can cause soft stems and rot. Place plant in location with good air circulation. Watch for whiteflies, mealybugs and aphids.

Bolivian Jew
Callisia repens
(kal-IS-ee-uh REE-penz)

Bolivian Jew

Light: Indirect or bright, diffused light.

Water: Moderately moist soil. Water thoroughly when just the soil surface is dry to the touch. Do not allow plants to stand in water.

Temperature: Moderate – 65-70°F days and 60-65°F nights.

Bolivian Jew is easy to grow and an excellent choice for hanging containers because its compact trailing growth cascades over the pot. Under favorable light conditions, small, white flowers may appear. Bolivian Jew resembles the Tahitian Bridal Veil, but prefers its soil a little moister. It will not tolerate overwatering, but this is the only area of concern since it is generally not troubled by insects and thrives under average home conditions.

BROMELIADS
Silver Vase Bromeliad
Aechmea fasciata
(eek-MEE-ah fash-ee-ATE-ah)

Light: Bright light, but can be maintained for many weeks in lower light.

Water: Maintain soil on the dry side. Drench soil thoroughly, then allow it to become moderately dry before watering again. Keep water in the foliage-formed cup at all times.

Temperature: Moderate/Warm – 65-75°F days and 60-70°F nights.

This popular bromeliad retains its dramatic pink flower up to six months, blooming above its large banded, vase-shaped rosette of leaves. Keep water in the cup of the plant at all times, but maintain planting medium on the dry side to avoid crown rot. Crown rot is the result of excessive soil moisture due to overwatering or poor drainage. Scale can be a problem with bromeliads.

Silver Vase Bromeliad

Striped Blushing Bromeliad
Neoregelia carolinae 'Tricolor'
(nee-oh-ree-JELL-yah care-oh-LEEN-eye)

Light: Bright light, but can be maintained for many weeks in lower light.

Water: Maintain planting medium on the dry side. Drench medium thoroughly, then allow it to become moderately dry before watering again. Keep water in the foliage-formed cup at all times. Do not allow plant to stand in water.

Striped Blushing Bromeliad

Temperature: Moderate/Warm – 65-75°F days and 60-70°F nights.

This stunning bromeliad variety "blushes" on young upper leaves as it prepares to bloom. This color lasts up to a year. Keep water in the foliage-formed cup at all times to avoid crown rot. Crown rot is the result of excessive soil moisture due to overwatering or poor drainage. Watch for scale and mealybugs.

CACTUS PLANTS
Golden Barrel Cactus
Echinocactus grusonii
(ek-eye-no-KAK-tus grew-SO-nigh)

Light: Bright light, but can be maintained for many weeks in lower light.

Water: Maintain soil on the dry side. Drench soil thoroughly, then allow it to become moderately dry before watering again. Keep soil very dry during the winter. Water sparingly in winter months. Once every 4 weeks is sufficient. Increase watering frequency in spring and summer.

Golden Barrel Cactus

Temperature: Moderate/Warm – 65-75°F days and 60-70°F nights.

Golden barrel cactus is easy to grow and is one of the most popular cactus varieties available. Strong yellow spines decorate each rib of the plant, giving it a unique look. The spines give it its golden coloring. Barrel cacti prefer cool temperatures during the winter months (45-55°F). This cactus is susceptible to root rot.

Caladium
Caladium bicolor
Formerly known as Caladium hybrid hortulanum
(kuh-LAY-dee-um)

Light: Indirect or bright, diffused light outdoors, out of direct sun. Bright light, indoors.

Water: Maintain planting medium on the dry side. Drench medium thoroughly, then allow it to become moderately dry before watering again.

Temperature: Warm – 70-75°F days and 65-70°F nights.

Caladium

popular plants

Caladium have foliage that rivals flowers in color and beauty. Their colorful foliage display includes red, pink, silver, white and green. Usually available from March to August, they offer a bright, colorful accent that lasts for about 4-6 weeks. Leaf colors fade when these plants remain in low light for over 2 months. When placed outdoors, caladium do best in partial or full shade, planted in containers or ground beds. They prefer rich soil. Check regularly for red spider mites. If you wish to overwinter caladium tubers, reduce watering when foliage begins to shrivel in fall. When foliage is shriveled completely, remove tubers from soil. Knock away soil and dead tops; store in perlite or vermiculite at 50°F during the winter in a dark place. In the spring, replant in pots, bud side down, raise the temperature to 80°F and keep soil moderately moist. If placing outdoors, wait until soil temperatures have warmed before planting.

Column Cactus

Column Cactus
Cereus species
(SEE-ree-us)

Light: Bright light, but can be maintained for many weeks in lower light.

Water: Maintain the soil on the dry side. Drench soil thoroughly, then allow it to become moderately dry before watering again. Keep soil very dry during the fall and winter. Water sparingly in winter months. Once every 4 weeks is sufficient. Increase watering frequency in spring and summer.

Temperature: Moderate/Warm – 65-75°F days and 60-70°F nights.

Also known as Curiosity Plant, column cactus are easy to grow and come in many shapes and sizes. The larger forms are popular for interior decorating. Cereus are often used as the base for grafted cacti forms. They prefer a cooler temperature (50-55°F) during the winter months.

Calathea

Calathea species
(kal-uh-THEE-ah)

Calathea

Light: Indirect or bright, diffused light.

Water: Moderately moist soil. Water thoroughly when just the soil surface is dry to the touch. Do not allow plants to stand in water.

Temperature: Warm – 70-75°F days and 65-70°F nights.

Calathea are moderately easy to grow, but require some special attention for successful growth. Often confused with the marantas because of their similar leaf markings, Calathea have leaves that arise from the crown in tufts. The attractive patterns radiate diagonally from the midrib of the long, broad leaves. Calathea require a very high humidity level to prevent browning of the leaf tips. Too-high light, excess fertilizer and fluoride can also cause browning. Avoid overwatering or under watering.

Calceolaria

Calceolaria crenatiflora
(kal-see-oh-LAIR-ee-ah kren-ah-ti-FLOOR-ah)

Calceolaria

Light: Bright light.

Water: Moderately moist soil. Water thoroughly when just the soil surface is dry to the touch. Do not allow plants to stand in water.

Temperature: Cool – 60-65°F days and 55-60°F nights.

Calceolaria are normally available from January through May. The plant is also referred to as Pocketbook Plant because its speckled pouches resemble tiny handbags. Calceolaria feature vibrant colors including yellow, red, orange, bronze, and bicolors, often with dark speckles. Calceolaria will bloom for 3-4 weeks and should be discarded after blooming stops. Placing them in a cool location at night (55-60°F) prolongs blooming. This native of the cool, bright Andes of Chile does not enjoy warm, dark conditions. Flower stems will stretch until they can no longer support the blooms. Take care with watering; overwatering causes yellow leaves, under watering causes wilting, and water on the foliage can cause rot. Full, direct sun can burn the flowers. Keep away from ripening fruit, which produces ethylene gas and causes flower drop. Watch for aphids, whiteflies and spider mites.

popular plants

Cape Primrose

Cape Primrose
Streptocarpus hybrid hybridus
(strep-toe-KAR-pus)

Light: Indirect or bright, diffused light.

Water: Moderately moist soil. Water thoroughly when just the soil surface is dry to the touch. Do not allow plants to stand in water.

Temperature: Moderate – 65-70°F days and 60-65°F nights.

Streptocarpus, or cape primrose plants are commonly available from May through August and will rebloom periodically in proper light conditions. Their delicate, trumpet-shaped flowers rise from a rosette of long, quilted leaves. Cape primrose will flower continuously in a bright location. It flowers more profusely if it receives 14 hours of bright, diffused light. It has a short resting period in winter, when it requires cooler temperatures (55-60°F). Watch for aphids and mealybugs.

Cast Iron Plant

Cast Iron Plant
Aspidistra elatior
(as-pi-DIS-trah ee-LAY-tee-or)

Light: Low light.

Water: Moderately moist soil. Water thoroughly when just the soil surface is dry to the touch. Do not allow plants to stand in water.

Temperature: Moderate – 65-70°F days and 60-65°F nights.

The cast iron plant is very easy to grow and gets its common name from its ability to tolerate poor conditions such as low light, drafts, low humidity, and neglect in watering and dusting. Of course, its long, leathery leaves will be more attractive with proper care. Popular as a parlor plant at the turn of the century, it can be featured as a nostalgia plant. Because it is slow growing, it is not widely available. Variegated forms do exist, and the green and white stripes add interest to this sturdy plant. This species is one of the most cold-hardy of the indoor foliage plants. Watch for red spider mites.

Chenille Plant

Acalypha hispida
(ah-CAL-ee-fah HISS-pa-dah)

Chenille Plant

Light: Bright light.

Water: Moderately moist soil. Water thoroughly when just the soil surface is dry to the touch. Do not allow plants to stand in water.

Temperature: Moderate – 65-70°F days and 60-65°F nights.

Chenille plants are commonly available from March through August. The bright green foliage makes a good background for pendant flower spikes of bright red, or sometimes, creamy white or purple. Flower spikes can be up to 8 inches long and are shaped like woolly foxtails. It flowers periodically in proper growing conditions. It requires high humidity and fertilization every 6 weeks. When grown in hanging containers, chenille plant is an attractive yet unusual plant for patios and porches.

China Doll

Radermachera sinica
(rad-er-MA-cheer-ah sin-EE-see-ah)

China Doll

Light: Low light location.

Water: Moderately moist soil. Water thoroughly when just the soil surface is dry to the touch. Do not allow plants to stand in water.

Temperature: Cool/Moderate – 60-70°F days and 55-65°F nights.

China doll is easy to grow, but requires a little special attention. It is a hardy plant, but susceptible to iron deficiency and somewhat sensitive to root nematode. Sap may be irritating, avoid contact with skin. China doll experiences little trouble with mites or mealybugs.

CHINESE EVERGREENS

Light: Low light location.

Water: Moderately moist soil. Water thoroughly when just the soil surface is dry to the touch. Do not allow plants to stand in water.

Temperature: Warm – 70-75°F days and 65-70°F nights.

Chinese evergreen is also commonly referred to by its botanical name, Aglaonema. It is durable, easy to grow and will tolerate low light, dry air and moderately dry soil. It can even be grown in water. Often confused with dieffenbachia, aglaonema offers the potential bonus of calla-like flowers, which mature to small red berries. Remove overgrown shoots to encourage new growth and keep the plant bushy. Possible problems include scale and mealybugs, as well as root rot in poorly drained soil in cool temperatures.

Chinese Evergreen

Chinese Evergreen
Aglaonema commutatum
(ag-lay-oh-NEE-ma kom-yew-TAY-tum)

Delicate silver markings decorate dark green leaves. This slow-growing plant is one of the most tolerant of low light conditions indoors.

Chinese Evergreen Maria
Aglaonema commutatum 'Maria'
(ag-lay-oh-NEE-ma kom-yew-TAY-tum)

This slow-growing variety has dark green foliage with light green variegation. It is a shorter plant than 'Silver Queen'. Three variety names are used interchangeably for this plant: 'Emerald Beauty', 'Maria' and 'Esmerelda'.

Chinese Evergreen Maria

Chinese Evergreen Silver Queen

Aglaonema 'Silver Queen'
(ag-lay-oh-NEE-ma)

This variety boasts a bold pattern of silver markings that may fade in very low light. 'Silver Queen' is sensitive to damage from exposure. Avoid temperatures below 50-55°F even for a few hours.

Chinese Evergreen Silver Queen

Chrysanthemum

Chrysanthemum Hybrid morifolium
(kris-AN-theh-mum)

Light: Bright light.

Water: Moderately moist soil. Water thoroughly when just the soil surface is dry to the touch. Do not allow plants to stand in water.

Temperature: Moderate – 65-70°F days and 60-70°F nights.

Chrysanthemum

Mum, or chrysanthemum, blooms are available in several flower shapes including single, decorative, daisy, Fuji and spider types. Colors ranging from white, gold, yellow, pink and lavender to bronze, red and purple add to the popularity of this plant. Cool nights (50-60°F) help maximize bloom time of up to 3 weeks. If bought in bud stage, chrysanthemums need bright light near a sunny window to encourage the buds to open. Once in full bloom, they can tolerate lower light. However, yellow leaves and black flower centers indicate light is too low. Avoid direct, full sunlight, which can burn the flowers. Watch for spider mites, aphids and whiteflies.

Reflowering: Mums will not reflower in the home without alternating darkness/bright light treatment of 10-12 weeks. It is very difficult to do and not recommended. Whether or not a florist mum can be grown outdoors depends on its hardiness and the climate where it is planted. If you wish to attempt growing florist mums after the flowers fade, just maintain the plant inside until danger of frost is past. Cut back the stems to about 3-4 inches from soil level and then plant outdoors. It may flower during the fall or it may freeze before it can flower. For best results with mums outdoors, buy hardy garden mums that are bred for use outdoors and make lovely border plants.

Cineraria

Pericallis hybrida
Formerly known as Senecio x hybrids
(per-eh-KAL-es HI-bred-a)

Light: Indirect or bright, diffused.

Water: Keep soil moist, not soggy, at all times.

Temperature: Cool – 60-65°F days and 55-60°F nights.

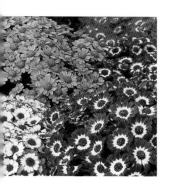

Cineraria

This beautiful native of the Canary Islands is an annual plant that is discarded after blooming. They are usually available from February through April, although supplies may vary slightly with individual growers. This plant is popular due to its wide range of bright colors including red, purple, blue, and salmon, some with white centers. Flowers last 1-3 weeks. Protect cineraria from full sunlight, which can scorch the flowers. They wilt easily in a cramped environment. Watch for aphids, whiteflies, and leaf miners.

CORN PLANTS

The corn plant is easy to grow. Improper watering may cause excessive tip burn and leaf drop, though occasional dropping of leaves is normal. Root rot and scale may also be problems. Avoid excessive fertilizer or high levels of boron or fluoride, which can cause leaf-tip burn.

Corn Plant

Dracaena fragrans
(drah-SEE-nah FRAY-granz)

Light: Indirect or bright, diffused light.

Water: Moderately moist soil. Water thoroughly when just the soil surface is dry to the touch. Do not allow plants to stand in water.

Corn Plant

Temperature: Warm – 70-75°F days and 65-70°F nights.

One of the most durable dracaenas, the corn plant gets its common name from the corn-like appearance of its foliage.

Striped Corn Plant

Dracaena fragrans 'Massangeana'
(drah-SEE-nah FRAY-granz)

Like its sister plant, the striped corn plant has leaves that resemble cornstalk foliage, but also features light green and yellow stripes running down the center of each leaf.

Striped Corn Plant

Crocus

Crocus vernus
(KROH-kus VER-nus)

Light: Indirect or bright, diffused light.

Water: Moderately moist soil. Water thoroughly when just the soil surface is dry to the touch. Do not allow plants to stand in water.

Temperature: Cool – 60-65°F days and 55-60°F nights.

Crocus are available from December through March and are typically the first blooms of spring. These cheerful flowers will bring the promise of spring into the home in late winter. Crocus bloom in lavender, purple, blue or white for approximately 1-2 weeks. Once forced to flower out of season, crocus corms cannot be forced indoors a second time. If you wish to plant the crocus in the garden, remove the flowers once they have faded.

Crocus

Keep the plant in a cool night location and continue watering until the foliage matures. Then, in late spring, move into the garden. It will bloom in 1-2 years during its normal spring blooming season.

Crossandra

Crossandra infundibuliformis
(kruh-SAND-rah in-fun-dih-bull-if-FOR-mus)

Light: Indirect or bright, diffused light.

Water: Moderately moist soil. Water thoroughly when just the soil surface is dry to the touch. Do not allow plants to stand in water.

Temperature: Warm – 70-75°F days and 65-70°F nights.

Also known as firecracker plant, crossandra is normally available in the spring and summer. This shrubby plant

Crossandra

has glossy leaves and overlapping flowers in clusters. Flowers range from salmon to orange in color and last from 3-4 weeks with periodic flowering. It prefers the warm, humid environment of its native India. Temperatures must not fall below 45°F or severe leaf drop can result. Dry conditions can cause leaf burn. Watch for whiteflies, which can be a severe problem.

Norma Croton

Codiaeum variegatum 'Norma'
(ko-dih-EE-um var-ee-ah-GAY-tum)

Light: Bright light, but can be maintained for many weeks in lower light.

Water: Moderately moist soil. Water thoroughly when just the soil surface is dry to the touch. Do not allow plants to stand in water.

Temperature: Warm – 70-75°F days and 65-70°F nights.

Norma Croton

The croton is easy to grow, but requires a little special attention. The spectacular colors of the waxy-leaved crotons range from yellow to orange, pink, copper, green and ivory. Older types may be difficult to grow in the north but many of the newer hybrids have been bred to tolerate lower light and other adverse conditions. Bright light enhances leaf color. Prune to promote bushy growth and watch for scale, mealybugs, and red spider mites.

Cyclamen

Cyclamen persicum
(SY-kla-men PER-sik-um)

Light: Indirect or bright, diffused light.

Water: Moderately moist soil. Water thoroughly when just the soil surface is dry to the touch. Do not allow plants to stand in water.

Temperature: Cool/Moderate – 60-70°F days and 55-65°F nights.

Cyclamen

Cyclamen are available primarily from October through April. They range in color from bright red, purple and pink to pastel shades of the same colors. Cyclamen will bloom continuously for 2-4 months with each blossom lasting 2-3 weeks. Plants must have bright, diffused light for the buds to develop and bloom above their spreading rosette of leaves. Cool nights (50-60°F) extend the flowering period. Watering-related problems include sudden leaf yellowing 1-2 days after wilting due to lack of water; this can also cause buds to shrivel and dry. High temperatures and low light can also damage buds. Be sure plant never stands in water and that there is no water in the crown at night, as this encourages rotting. Cyclamen mites can cause new leaves and flowers to become curled and deformed.

Reflowering: After flowering stops, cyclamen leaves will die down. During this time, gradually reduce watering and allow soil to become dry. When all top growth is gone, dig up the dry, beet-like corm and replant in fresh potting medium. The corm should be halfway out of the medium to prevent crown rot. Water well and place in a well-lit location. Second-year plants will have smaller flowers, but more blossoms.

Daffodil

Narcissus pseudonarcissus
(nar-SIS-is soo-doe-nar-SIS-us)

Light: Indirect or bright, diffused light.

Water: Moderately moist soil. Water thoroughly when just the soil surface is dry to the touch. Do not allow plants to stand in water.

Temperature: Cool – 60-65°F days and 55-60°F nights.

Daffodils are generally available from February through April. Daffodils are all part of the large Narcissus genus. They range from the traditional all-yellow varieties to various white and golden varieties; some with contrasting trumpets, some with trumpets rimmed in orange. Daffodils will bloom for 1-2 weeks.

Daffodil

Reflowering: Bulbs cannot be reflowered indoors once they have been forced out of season. Remove the flowers after they have faded, keep the plant in its cool night location and continue watering until the foliage matures. In late spring, plant in the garden. It will bloom in 1-2 years during its normal spring blooming season.

Dieffenbachia

DIEFFENBACHIA PLANTS

Light: Indirect or bright, diffused light.

Water: Maintain soil on the dry side. Drench soil thoroughly, then allow it to become moderately dry before watering again.

Temperature: Warm – 70-75°F days and 65-70°F nights.

Dieffenbachia maintain their popularity as a houseplant because of their beauty, variety and ease and speed of growing. As they mature, there is a normal dropping of lower leaves to reveal an attractive trunk-like stalk. Overwatering and stem rot are common problems, especially at low temperatures. Watch for mites and mealybugs. Dieffenbachia sap causes mouth tissues to swell if chewed, so keep out of reach of small children and pets.

Dieffenbachia Maculata

Dieffenbachia maculata 'Exotica Compacta'
(deef-en-BOCK-ee-uh mack-you-LAY-tah)

This popular version of dieffenbachia has more compact growing characteristics than other varieties. It is perfect for areas of the home or office where space is limited.

Camille Dieffenbachia

Camille Dieffenbachia

Dieffenbachia maculata 'Camille'
(deef-en-BOCK-ee-uh mack-you-LAY-tah)

This self-branching variety is typified by bright yellow variegation on the leaves. It is a bushy variety with few problems and is very popular.

Tropic Snow Dieffenbachia

Dieffenbachia amoena 'Tropic Snow'
(deef-en-BOCK-ee-uh uh-MEE-nah)

This sturdy plant bears wide, spreading, dark green leaves blotched in creamy white along the veins. Due to lesser variegation, it will tolerate lower light levels than most dieffenbachia.

Tropic Snow Dieffenbachia

DRACAENA PLANTS
Gold-Dust Dracaena
Dracaena surculosa
(drah-SEE-nah sir-cuh-LOW-sah)

Gold-Dust Dracaena

Light: Indirect or bright, diffused light.

Water: Moderately moist soil. Water thoroughly when just the soil surface is dry to the touch. Do not allow plants to stand in water.

Temperature: Warm – 70-75°F days and 65-70°F nights.

Gold-Dust dracaena is easy to grow, but requires a little special attention. Improper watering may cause excessive tip burn and leaf drop, though occasional dropping of leaves is normal. Root rot and scale may also be problems. Avoid excessive fertilizer or high levels of boron or fluoride, which can cause leaf-tip burn.

This small, shrub-like variety has a growth habit different from its other dracaena relatives. Its numerous creamy-gold splotches make it a standout in dish gardens. It's a slow-growing plant.

Janet Craig Dracaena
Dracaena deremensis 'Janet Craig'
(drah-SEE-nah dare-eh-MEN-sis)

Janet Craig Dracaena

Light: Indirect or bright, diffused light.

Water: Moderately moist soil. Water thoroughly when just the soil surface is dry to the touch. Do not allow plants to stand in water.

Temperature: Warm – 70-75°F days and 65-70°F nights.

The Janet Craig dracaena is easy to grow. Improper watering may cause excessive tip burn and leaf drop, though occasional dropping of leaves is normal. Root rot and scale may also be problems. Avoid excessive fertilizer or high levels of boron or fluoride, which can cause leaf-tip burn.

The dark green, glossy leaf blades of this variety are stiffly corrugated. It's a durable, slow-growing beauty.

Red Margin Dracaena

Red Margin Dracaena
Dracaena cincta
Formerly known as Dracaena marginata
(drah-SEE-nah SINK-ta)

Light: Indirect or bright, diffused light.

Water: Moderately moist soil. Water thoroughly when just the soil surface is dry to the touch. Do not allow plants to stand in water.

Temperature: Warm – 70-75°F days and 65-70°F nights.

The red margin dracaena is easy to grow, but requires a little special attention. Improper watering may cause excessive tip burn and leaf drop, though occasional dropping of leaves is normal. Root rot and scale may also be problems. Avoid excessive fertilizer or high levels of boron or fluoride, which can cause leaf-tip burn.

This dramatic tropical tree boasts striking rosettes of long, narrow leaves with red margins on slender, interesting trunks.

Warneckei Dracaena
Dracaena deremensis 'Warneckei'
(drah-SEE-nah dare-eh-MEN-sis)

Light: Indirect or bright, diffused light.

Water: Moderately moist soil. Water thoroughly when just the soil surface is dry to the touch. Do not allow plants to stand in water.

Temperature: Warm – 70-75°F days and 65-70°F nights.

The Warneckei dracaena is easy to grow. Improper watering may cause excessive tip burn and leaf drop, though occasional dropping of leaves is normal. Root rot and scale may also be problems. Avoid excessive fertilizer or high levels of boron or fluoride, which can cause leaf-tip burn.

The sword-shaped leaves of Warneckei are decorated with fine white stripes down the center and near the edge. This is another easy-care, durable dracaena.

Warneckei Dracaena

English Primrose
Primula vulgaris
(PRIM-you-lah vul-GAY-ris)

Light: Indirect or bright, diffused light.

Water: Moderately moist soil. Water thoroughly when just the soil surface is dry to the touch. Do not allow plants to stand in water.

Temperature: Cool – 60-65°F days and 55-60°F nights.

English primrose are available from January through April. Many hybrids of this native European perennial have been developed especially as attractive pot plants.

English Primrose

Green, quilted leaves form a rosette and contrast nicely with the colorful flowers. Flower colors include red, yellow, orange, maroon, blue, white and purple, often with contrasting eye. Flowers bloom for 1-3 weeks. English primrose will not generally flower again indoors, but it can be planted outdoors in spring in a shaded location where it will flower in subsequent years during late spring and early summer.

FERNS
Bird's Nest Fern
Asplenium nidus
(as-PLEE-ni-um NYE-dus)

Light: Indirect or bright, diffused light.

Water: Keep soil very moist, but not soggy, at all times.

Temperature: Moderate – 65-70°F days and 60-65°F nights.

The unique bird's nest fern gets its name from the nest-like "hairs" in its crown from which the fronds rise. It is one of the easiest ferns to grow because it will tolerate lower humidity and drier soils. It is possible for excessive humidity in cooler temperatures to cause the fronds to turn brown; however, this humidity level is highly unlikely in the home environment. Keep water out of the crown of

Bird's Nest Fern

the plant to prevent rotting. Though it thrives in moderate temperatures, it prefers cooler nights. Do not buy a plant with water-soaked appearance, tissue deterioration, brown patched at leaf base or streaks in the leaves. Bird's nest fern is susceptible to foliar nematodes (minute, wormlike organisms).

Boston Fern

Nephrolepis exaltata 'Bostoniensis'
(nee-FROW-lep-is eks-al-TAY-tah)

Light: Indirect or bright, diffused light.

Water: Moderately moist soil. Water thoroughly when just the soil surface is dry to the touch. Do not allow plants to stand in water.

Temperature: Moderate – 65-70°F days and 60-65°F nights.

The Boston fern is easy to grow, but requires a little special attention. When you say "fern," the popular Boston fern is the image that comes to mind. This plant is most popular because of its relative ease of growing and its elegant, graceful growth habit, either hanging or standing. Humidity is its only troublesome requirement. Bright, dry conditions will cause yellowing and browning of the fronds. Watch for scale and mealybugs and place your fern out of traffic areas, since a frond will not grow back once it is broken. This Victorian favorite has long, pendant fronds up to 3 feet with flat, closely set leaflets.

Boston Fern

Dallas Fern

Nephrolepis exaltata 'Dallasii'
(nee-FROW-lep-is eks-al-TAY-tah)

Light: Low light.

Water: Moderately moist soil. Water thoroughly when just the soil surface is dry to the touch. Do not allow plants to stand in water.

Temperature: Moderate – 65-70°F days and 60-65°F nights.

The Dallas fern is easy to grow As a member of the genus Nephrolepis, it exhibits the same elegant, graceful growth habit as the Boston fern. The Dallas fern is considerably smaller in scale though and it's ideal for tabletop or hanging basket. It also tolerates low humidity and temperature extremes of 50-90°F, making it extremely well suited to low light situations.

Dallas Fern

Fluffy Ruffles Fern
Nephrolepis exaltata 'Fluffy Ruffles'
(nee-FROW-lep-is eks-al-TAY-tah)

Light: Indirect or bright, diffused light.

Water: Moderately moist soil. Water thoroughly when just the soil surface is dry to the touch. Do not allow plants to stand in water.

Temperature: Moderate – 65-70°F days and 60-65°F nights.

Fluffy Ruffles fern is another of the popular ferns from the genus Nephrolepis. It is easy to grow and exhibits the same elegant, graceful growth habit of the Boston fern. Humidity is its only troublesome requirement. Bright, dry conditions will cause yellowing and browning of the fronds. Watch for scale and mealybugs and place your fern out of traffic areas, since a frond will not grow back once it is broken.

Fluffy Ruffles Fern

The Fluffy Ruffles cultivar has dense fronds which exhibit tightly gathered, fine leaflets that give the plant a ruffled appearance.

Maidenhair Fern
Adiantum raddianum
(ad-ee-AN-tum rad-ee-AN-um)

Light: Low light location.

Water: Keep soil very moist, but not soggy, at all times.

Temperature: 70-75°F days and 65-75°F nights.

The delicate maidenhair fern is a challenge to grow because of its care requirements. It prefers a highly organic soil supplement with peat moss or shredded bark. It will not tolerate dry soil, especially in high temperatures, and is sensitive to wet soil in low temperatures. High humidity (70-80%) is necessary to prevent curling and browning of leaflets. Do not spray water on foliage. Aphids, whiteflies, mealybugs and scale may be a problem. Maidenhair fern is also susceptible to insecticide damage. Do not use malathion.

Maidenhair Fern
FLORAMEDIA®

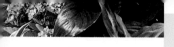

Sprengeri Asparagus
Fern

Sprengeri Asparagus Fern
Asparagus densiflorus 'Sprengeri'
(as-PARE-uh-gus den-se-FLOOR-us)

Light: Indirect or bright, diffused light.

Water: Moderately moist soil. Water thoroughly when just the soil surface is dry to the touch. Do not allow plants to stand in water.

Temperature: Cool/Moderate – 60-70°F days and 55-65°F nights.

The Sprengeri asparagus fern is easy to grow, but requires a little special attention. The distinctive asparagus fern cascades in a delicate veil of fluffy branchlets, with narrow leaves reduced to the shape of needles. It is not a true fern. Though its preferred growing conditions are easy to attain, it is a sensitive plant and drops "needles" readily if overwatered or in inadequate light. Tolerates brighter light. It can be sensitive to some insecticides, too, so treat sparingly if red spider mites attack. Sprengeri asparagus fern is an attractive accent when used with other plants in container gardens.

Staghorn Fern

Staghorn Fern
Platycerium species
(plat-ih-SEE-rih-um)

Light: Indirect or bright, diffused light.

Water: Moderately moist soil. Water thoroughly when just the medium's surface is dry to the touch. Do not allow plants to stand in water.

Temperature: Moderate/Warm – 65-75°F days and 60-70°F nights.

This unique, dramatic staghorn fern is truly striking mounted on the wall like a trophy. It is moderately easy to grow, but has some special requirements for success. It has a large, sterile frond and short, lobed spore-bearing fronds resembling a stag's horn. In nature, it

grows on the bark of trees so it is usually grown on bark or in peat moss rather than in soil. Allow plenty of growth space. Humidity is a special concern with staghorns. It tends to dry out quickly, especially when mounted on the wall. It should be misted and the growing medium soaked regularly.
Fertilize only sparingly; too much fertilizer is harmful.

Fiddleleaf Fig

Ficus lyrata
(FYE-kus lye-RAY-tah)

Light: Indirect or bright, diffused light.

Water: Moderately moist soil. Water thoroughly when just the soil surface is dry to the touch. Do not allow plants to stand in water.

Temperature: Warm – 70-75°F days and 65-70°F nights.

The fiddleleaf fig is easy to grow. Ficus are generally durable and grow best in small containers, so repotting is seldom necessary. Named for its large, waxy fiddle-shaped leaves, the fiddleleaf fig is a bit more sensitive than its rubber plant relatives. It may drop leaves in low light and get brown leaf spots if overwatered. Watch for red spider mites, scale, and mealybugs.

Fiddleleaf Fig

White Fittonia

Fittonia verschaffeltii argyroneura
(fit-OH-nee-ah ver-shaf-EL-tee-eye are-ji-row-NUR-uh)

Light: Indirect or bright, diffused light.

Water: Moderately moist soil. Water thoroughly when just the soil surface is dry to the touch. Do not allow plants to stand in water.

Temperature: Warm – 70-75°F days and 65-70°F nights.

This delicate fittonia is lovely with its intricate pattern of white veins against bright green leaves, but a challenge to grow because of its high humidity requirements and water sensitivity. Avoid chilling temperatures. Do not allow the plant to wilt. A covered terrarium is a good environment, but be sure to avoid high light. Watch for whiteflies, mealybugs and slugs, which are snail-like organisms that make large holes in the leaves.

White Fittonia

Gardenia

Gardenia

Gardenia augusta   *Also known as Gardenia jasminoides*
(gar-DEEN-ya aw-GUS-ta)

Light: Bright light.

Water: Moderately moist soil. Water thoroughly when just the soil surface is dry to the touch. Do not allow plants to stand in water.

Temperature: Warm – 70-75°F days and 62-65°F nights.

The elegant gardenia is unmatched for beauty and fragrance, but it is difficult to grow in home environments. It's commonly available January through May, in both white and cream flower varieties. In the right environment, blossoms will last 3-8 days. The gardenia is intolerant of temperature shifts, preferring 70°F days and 62-65°F nights. Night temperatures below 62°F will cause yellowing foliage. Night temperatures above 65°F reduce growth of lower buds and increase the chance of bud abortion. Bud abortion is also caused by drafts, inconsistent watering and lack of humidity. Gardenias prefer very high humidity (70-75%). Alkaline soil can also cause yellow leaves, so use an acid-based fertilizer regularly. Watch for mealybugs, scale and spider mites.

Martha Washington Geranium

Pelargonium hybrid domesticum
(pel-ar-GO-nee-um HI-brid doe-MES-ti-cum)

Light: Bright light.

Water: Maintain soil on the dry side. Drench soil thoroughly, then allow it to become moderately dry before watering again.

Temperature: Cool – 60-65°F days and 55-60°F nights.

Martha Washington Geranium

The Martha Washington geranium is generally available from April through June. This distinctive geranium has interesting leaves with sawtooth edges and comes in a wide range of colors including white, pink, purple, red and salmon, many with accents of color. Martha Washington geraniums will flower up to 4 weeks if cared for properly.

They prefer the cooler days of early summer. Foliage is attractive when plant is not in flower. Diseases can be a problem, particularly if the plant is overwatered.

Gerbera Daisy

Gerbera jamesonii
(GER-ber-rah jay-ma-SO-nee-eye)

Light: Bright light.

Water: Moderately moist soil. Water thoroughly when just the soil surface is dry to the touch. Do not allow plants to stand in water.

Temperature: Moderate – 65-70°F days and 60-65°F nights.

Gerbera Daisy

The Gerbera daisy is commonly available from March through July. Daisy-like flowers can be single, double, quilled or crested double on long stems. They are available in a variety of colors including shades of orange, red, yellow, white and pink. Gerbera daisies will flower continuously for 4-6 weeks with proper care. Although they are perennial in very warm climates, they are generally treated as an annual. Over watering will cause crown rot. Watch for whiteflies.

Giant White Inch Plant

Tradescantia albiflora 'Albovittata'
(trah-des-CAN-she-ah al-bih-FLOR-ah)

Light: Indirect or bright, diffused light.

Water: Maintain soil on the dry side. Drench soil thoroughly, then allow it to become moderately dry before watering again.

Temperature: Moderate – 65-70°F days and 60-65°F nights.

The giant white inch plant is easy to grow. It is a vigorous hanging plant that stays bushier and more attractive if pruned regularly. The resulting cuttings root easily in rooting medium or water. Giant white inch can be grown indefinitely in water. In soil, however, it is sensitive to overwatering as well as red spider mites.

Giant White Inch Plant

White stripes decorate the bluish-green leaves of the inch plant. Remove stems that produce all-green or all-white leaves. The green ones can become dominant and take over the plant, while the white ones sap the plant's strength because they have no chlorophyll for their own photosynthesis. Sometimes mistaken for wandering Jew.

Gloxinia
Sinningia speciosa
(sin-IN-jee-ah spee-see-OH-sah)

Light: Indirect or bright, diffused light.

Water: Moderately moist soil. Water thoroughly when just the soil surface is dry to the touch. Do not allow plants to stand in water.

Temperature: Warm – 70-75°F days and 65-70°F nights.

The popular gloxinia plant is available all year, but is very common from March through November. The luxurious, velvety gloxinia blossom comes in lush shades of red, pink, purple and bicolors. The attractive blossoms will last from 2-4 weeks with proper care. Gloxinia need bright light for new buds to develop and open. Low light will result in small, pale flowers. Take care not to overwater, as this can prevent buds from developing. Avoid splashing water on the leaves, which can cause yellow spots. They are generally pest resistant, but are sometimes bothered by aphids and thrips.

Reflowering: After flowering, gloxinia will die back and require a period of dormancy. Withhold water and fertilizer and keep it in continuous darkness for 6-8 weeks. Repot the tubers at soil level in a very porous soil mix. Water sparingly and return to the light. Resume normal watering and fertilization levels as soon as new growth appears. Gloxinia flower in about 3 months from tubers.

Gloxinia

Fiona Grape Ivy
Cissus rhombifolia 'Fiona'
(SIS-us rom-bih-FOE-lee-uh)

Light: Indirect or bright, diffused light.

Water: Moderately moist soil. Water thoroughly when just the soil surface is dry to the touch. Do not allow plants to stand in water.

Temperature: Moderate/Warm – 65-75°F days and 60-70°F nights.

Fiona Grape Ivy

Grape ivy is easy to grow. The Cissus cultivars are among the fastest growing ivies. Tough and tolerant of low humidity and occasional watering neglect, they're ideal for the plant novice. Their curling tendrils can cling to supports or they will cascade in a tumble of hanging foliage. Spider mites can be a problem. Overwatering may cause leaves to yellow, and low light will cause new leaves to grow smaller.

Hawaiian Ti

Cordyline terminalis 'Baby Doll'
(core-dih-LEE-nee ter-min-AH-lis)

Light: Indirect or bright, diffused light.

Water: Moderately moist soil. Water thoroughly when just the soil surface is dry to the touch. Do not allow plants to stand in water.

Temperature: Moderate/Warm – 65-75°F days and 60-70°F nights.

The Hawaiian Ti is easy to grow, but requires a little special attention. Often confused with the dracaenas, Hawaiian Ti

Hawaiian Ti

has more color variety that ranges from red to pink, cream, copper, and green in good light conditions. These colorful leaves have a palm-like appearance when mature. High humidity is the only difficult requirement. Hawaiian Ti may lose its lower leaves due to dry air, hot temperatures or low light. Watch for red spider mites and avoid superphosphate in the soil mix, since it can cause leaf-tip burn due to its fluoride content.

Heliconia

Heliconia sp.
(hel-li-KO-ni-a)

Light: Bright light, but can be maintained for many weeks in lower light.

Water: Moderately moist soil. Water thoroughly when just the soil surface is dry to the touch. Do not allow plants to stand in water.

Temperature: Warm – 70-75°F days and 65-70°F nights.

Heliconia is easy to grow, but requires a little special attention. Heliconia has been called the "fake bird-of-

Heliconia

paradise" because its flowers resemble the ornamental bird-of-paradise. It has few insect problems and is disease resistant. Poor drainage can cause root problems.

Heliconia will hold all of the flowers that are already formed when the plant is taken indoors.

Hibiscus

Hibiscus rosa-sinensis
(hy-BIS-cus RO-sa si-NEN-sis)

Light: Bright light.

Water: Moderately moist soil. Water thoroughly when just the soil surface is dry to the touch. Do not allow plants to stand in water.

Temperature: Moderate/Warm – 65-75°F days and 60-70°F nights.

Hibiscus

Hibiscus are available all year. The exotic hibiscus has large single or double flowers that last only a day. Colors range from rose, purple, pink and red to yellow, orange and white. They will flower continuously with proper care, and are long-lived plants. Decorative blossoms will last all day, even without water. Bud drop is a problem caused by low light, cold temperatures, overheating or drying out. Keep continuously moist to avoid wilting. Watch for aphids, spider mites and whiteflies.

Hyacinth

Hyacinthus orientalis
(HY-ah-SINTH-us or-ee-en-TAY-lis)

Light: Indirect or bright, diffused light.

Water: Moderately moist soil. Water thoroughly when just the soil surface is dry to the touch. Do not allow plants to stand in water.

Temperature: Cool – 60-65°F days and 55-60°F nights.

Hyacinth

Hyacinths are available from December through April. Fragrant spikes of flowers will bring spring to the home early, lasting from 1-2 weeks with proper care. Hyacinths are available in white, red, violet, blue and pink.

Reflowering: Bulbs will not rebloom indoors once they have been forced out of season. Keep the plant in a cool location at night, remove the flowers after they have faded, and continue watering until the foliage matures. In late spring, plant in the garden. It will bloom in 1-2 years in its normal spring blooming season.

Hydrangea

Hydrangea macrophylla
(hy-DRAIN-ja mak-row-FIL-ah)

Light: Bright light.

Water: Keep soil very moist, but not soggy, at all times.

Temperature: Moderate – 65-70°F days and 60-65°F nights.

The striking hydrangea is available from March through May. Large "snowballs" of pink, blue or white blossoms will last from 1-3 weeks with proper care. The plant is very sensitive to wilting. Soil that is too alkaline causes

Hydrangea

yellow leaves. Blue flowers are produced by adding iron or aluminum sulfate to the soil. Soil pH levels are also important in determining flower color. Pink blossoms require a soil pH of 6.0, and blue blooms a soil pH of 5.5. Under natural growing conditions, blue-flowering plants revert to pink. Cool night temperatures (50-60°F) help extend the blooming period.

Reflowering: Trying to reflower hydrangeas indoors is very difficult and not recommended. In areas where winter temperatures do not fall below 0°F, they can be planted outdoors and will bloom each summer.

Ivy

Hedera helix species
(HEAD-er-ah HEE-lix)

Light: Bright light, but can be maintained for many weeks in lower light.

Water: Moderately moist soil. Water thoroughly when just the soil surface is dry to the touch. Do not allow plants to stand in water.

Temperature: Cool/Moderate – 60-70°F days and 55-65°F nights.

Ivy

Trailing hedera ivies are popular and easy to grow but require a little special attention. The variegated varieties require higher light than the all-green varieties. Hedera don't like hot temperatures, particularly when accompanied by dry soil, which will cause browning of the growing tip. High temperatures also make hedera more susceptible to attack from red spider mites and scale.

Jade Plant
Crassula species
(CRASS-you-lah)

Jade Plant

Light: Bright light, but can be maintained for many weeks in lower light.

Water: Maintain soil on the dry side. Drench soil thoroughly, then allow it to become moderately dry before watering again.

Temperature: Warm – 70-75°F days and 65-70°F nights.

The jade plant is easy to grow. Crassula vary in appearance but all are succulents. Avoid overwatering and low light conditions. Watch for mealybugs.

Jerusalem Cherry
Solanum pseudocapsicum
(soh-LAY-num soo-doe-CAP-sik-um)

Jerusalem Cherry
FLORAMEDIA®

Light: Bright light.

Water: Maintain soil on the dry side. Drench soil thoroughly, then allow it to become moderately dry before watering again.

Temperature: Moderate – 65-70°F days and 60-65°F nights.

The Jerusalem cherry is available from September through January, but is most popular in November and December. It is prized for its decorative, bright orange "cherries" that follow tiny, white star-like flowers. The fruit ripens from green to yellow to red and lasts from 1-2 months. Although related to the tomato and potato, this fruit is not edible and may be harmful to some individuals. Keep away from small children. Leaf drop may occur due to low light or lack of humidity. Watch for whiteflies and spider mites.

Reflowering: After fruit is gone, cut plant back to 2-3 inches. Pinch growing tips through June to encourage branching, then allow plant to flower in summer. Fruits will form after flowering, and plant should be brought indoors to prevent frost damage in the fall. After danger of frost is past, Jerusalem cherry may be grown outdoors.

Kalanchoe

Kalanchoe blossfeldiana
(kal-an-KOH-ee [or ka-LAN-cho] blos-feld-ee-AH-nah)

Light: Bright light.

Water: Maintain soil on the dry side. Drench soil thoroughly, then allow it to become moderately dry before watering again.

Temperature: Moderate – 65-70°F days and 60-65°F nights.

Kalanchoe are available all year, but are most popular March through September. These colorful succulents retain decorative value as interesting foliage plants after

Kalanchoe

the flowers have faded. Flowers come in shades of red, pink, salmon, white, orange and yellow, and last from 2-6 weeks. Bright light is necessary to sustain the flower colors. Pale or bicolored flowers indicate inadequate light. Avoid overwatering, as this can encourage crown rot and powdery mildew.

Reflowering: To reflower, kalanchoe require 14 hours of continuous darkness followed by 10 hours of bright light for a period of 6 weeks to initiate and develop buds. The buds formed during this time will continue to develop during normal indoor light conditions after the 6-week treatment, but flowering will not occur until 3-4 months after.

Easter Lily

Lilium longiflorum
(LIL-ee-um lon-jih-FLOR-um)

Light: Indirect or bright, diffused light.

Water: Moderately moist soil. Water thoroughly when just the soil surface is dry to the touch. Do not allow plants to stand in water.

Easter Lily

Temperature: Moderate – 65-70°F days and 50-60°F nights.

This stately white lily is a classic symbol of Easter and is available in March or April, depending on when the holiday falls. The fragrant white flowers will bloom continuously for 1-2 weeks. Blooms will last longer if the plant is placed in a cool location (50-60°F) at night. You may remove the yellow anthers to prevent pollen from staining the pure white blooms. Watch for aphids.

Reflowering: After flowering, keep pot in a well-lit location and continue watering as foliage matures. In late spring, set entire plant into the garden. It will reflower the following summer.

Hybrid Asiatic Lily

Lilium hybrid
(LIL-ee-um)

Light: Indirect or bright, diffused light.

Water: Moderately moist soil. Water thoroughly when just the soil surface is dry to the touch. Do not allow plants to stand in water.

Temperature: Moderate – 65-70°F days and 50-60°F nights.

Many colorful varieties of hybrid lilies are available to provide a vivid change of pace from the standard white Easter lily. Hybrid lilies are commonly available from March through May and come in many colorful varieties including pink, red, peach, yellow, bronze and white. Most species originated in Asia, but were hybridized in the U.S. Some have contrasting speckles. Plants will bloom from 1-2 weeks. Blooms will last longer if the plant is placed in a cool location (50-60°F) at night. You may remove the anthers to prevent pollen from staining the blooms. Watch for aphids.

Reflowering: After flowering, keep pot in a well-lit location and continue watering as foliage matures. In late spring, set entire plant into the garden. It will reflower the following summer.

Hybrid Asiatic Lily

Nephthytis

Syngonium podophyllum 'White Butterfly'
(sin-GOH-nee-um poh-doh-FILL-um)

Light: Indirect or bright, diffused light.

Water: Moderately moist soil. Water thoroughly when just the soil surface is dry to the touch. Do not allow plants to stand in water.

Temperature: Warm – 70-75°F days and 65-70°F nights.

Nephthytis is easy to grow. Its pointed but young leaves become lobed and divide into five to nine segments as the plant matures, and its form changes from upright to trailing. To keep growth compact, limit water and nitrogen. The creamy pale color of this variegated variety will become darker and less attractive in low light. Watch for mealybugs.

Nephthytis

Norfolk Island Pine

Araucaria heterophylla
(air-ah-CARE-ee-ah het-er-oh-FILE-uh)

Light: Indirect or bright, diffused light.

Water: Moderately moist soil. Water thoroughly when just the soil surface is dry to the touch. Do not allow plants to stand in water.

Temperature: Moderate – 65-70°F days and 60-65°F nights.

The Norfolk Island pine is easy to grow, but requires a little special attention. This dramatic evergreen plant is often used as a living Christmas tree. In its natural environment it grows very large, but as a houseplant it is slow-growing and will not outgrow the average home environment for many years. It prefers a soil rich in humus. It may need staking as it grows taller and should be turned frequently to keep growth symmetrical if light comes from only one direction. Low light, improper watering, low humidity or high temperature may cause branches to become brittle, turn brown and drop. Watch for red spider mites.

Norfolk Island Pine

Oak Leaf Ivy
Cissus rhombifolia 'Ellen Danica'
(SIS-us rom-bih-FOE-lee-uh)

Light: Indirect or bright, diffused light.

Water: Moderately moist soil. Water thoroughly when just the soil surface is dry to the touch. Do not allow plants to stand in water.

Temperature: Moderate/Warm – 65-75°F days and 60-70°F nights.

Oak Leaf Ivy

Oak leaf ivy is easy to grow. The Cissus cultivars are among the fastest-growing ivies. Tough and tolerant of low humidity and occasional watering neglect, they're ideal for the plant novice. Their curling tendrils can cling to supports or they will cascade in a tumble of hanging foliage. Spider mites can be a problem. Overwatering may cause leaves to turn yellow, and low light will result in smaller leaves.

This durable variety displays bushy, climbing or hanging stems of lobed leaves that resemble oak leaves.

ORCHIDS

Light: Indirect or bright, diffused light.

Water: Moderately moist soil. Water generously when growing; water less often when plant is dormant. Do not allow plants to stand in water or completely dry out.

Orchid, Cymbidium
Cymbidium sp.
(sim-BID-ee-um)

Orchid, Cymbidium

Temperature: Cool – 65-70°F days and 50-55°F nights.

Cymbidium orchids grow on branching sprays in a range of colors, including shades of white, yellow, green, pink and bicolors. This orchid flowers in early spring. Avoid getting flowers wet when watering. The cymbidium orchid plant prefers high humidity (60-70%) and good air circulation. Repot every 2-3 years, in leafy, well-drained soil. Take care not to disturb the roots, as this will delay flowering. This orchid requires a cooling period to initiate buds; 45-50°F for 3-5 weeks in the fall.

Orchid, Dendrobium
Dendrobium sp.
(den-DRO-bee-um)

Temperature: Warm – 75-80°F days and 68-75°F nights.

Dendrobium orchids bloom in a rainbow of colors including white, yellow, pink and bicolors. It flowers in winter, spring or summer depending on the variety. Avoid getting flowers wet when watering. Prefers high humidity (60-70%) and good air circulation. Grows best when slightly pot bound, but when repotting is necessary, plant in an orchid mix (bark, coconut fiber, etc.). Dendrobium orchids are a highly varied genus and specific care requirements vary with species.

Orchid, Dendrobium

Orchid, Phalaenopsis
Phalaenopsis sp.
(fail-eh-NOP-sis)

Light: Indirect or bright, diffused light.

Water: Evenly moist soil. Do not allow plants to stand in water or dry out completely.

Temperature: Warm – 75-80°F days and 68-75°F nights.

Phalaenopsis orchids feature elegant moth-shaped flowers that bloom in fall, winter or spring, depending on variety, in many striking colors. Lower temperatures

Orchid, Phalaenopsis

(60°F) in fall will produce more flowers. The phalaenopsis orchid plant prefers high humidity (60-70%) and good air circulation. Avoid sudden, drastic changes in temperature. Repot in coarse orchid mix (bark, coconut fiber, etc.) about every 18 months or when medium has deteriorated. Be sure to cut away any brown roots.

Ornamental Pepper
Capsicum annuum
(KAP-sik-um AHN-you-um)

Light: Bright light.

Water: Moderately moist soil. Water thoroughly when just the soil surface is dry to the touch. Do not allow plants to stand in water.

Temperature: Warm – 70-75°F days and 65-70°F nights.

Ornamental peppers are tropical shrubs related to the tomato and potato. They are generally available July through December, most commonly in August, September, and October as a potted plant. Also available in spring for bedding. The plant will last from 1-3 months depending on the cultivar and care, and should be discarded when no longer attractive. They do well in the increased light and air circulation of porch or patio. Ornamental fruit ripens from green to yellow, orange, red and purple. The decorative fruit is usually edible but extremely hot. Wilting can be a problem, causing foliage loss. Watch for red spider mites, aphids and whiteflies.

Ornamental Pepper

PALMS

Light: Indirect or bright, diffused light.

Water: Moderately moist soil. Water thoroughly when just the soil surface is dry to the touch. Do not allow plants to stand in water.

Temperature: Warm – 70-75°F days and 65-70°F nights.

Unless otherwise indicated, most palms prefer the above light, water and temperature requirements.

Areca Palm
Chrysalidocarpus lutescens
(kris-al-is-oh-KAR-pus loo-TES-enz)

Light: Bright light, but can be maintained for many weeks in lower light.

Water: Moderately moist soil. Water thoroughly when just the soil surface is dry to the touch. Do not allow plants to stand in water.

Temperature: Warm – 70-75°F days and 65-70°F nights.

The areca palm is easy to grow, but requires a little special attention. The elegant palm has attractive yellow stems that become bamboo-like on older plants. The

Areca Palm

clumps of graceful foliage can grow quite large, with mature fronds up to 2-3 feet long. Watch for red spider mites, scale, and mealybugs. Watering maintenance may be a problem also. Plants must not be allowed to dry out, which may happen rapidly in high temperatures.

Bamboo Palm
Chamaedorea erumpens
(kam-uh-DOR-ee-ah ee-RUM-penz)

The bamboo palm is easy to grow. This clustering palm adds graceful elegance to home décor. Common problems are yellowing leaves or browning tips due to improper watering. Overwatering will cause root rot. Watch for red spider mites, scale and mealybugs.

Bamboo Palm

Chinese Fan Palm
Livistona chinensis
(liv-iss-TONE-ah chin-EN-sis)

The Chinese fan palm is easy to grow, but requires special attention. The glossy fan-shaped leaves of this impressive palm can grow over 5 feet across. Each fan is cut into many narrow, single-ribbed segments that split again at the tips to form a fringe. The long leaf stems have small spines at the tips when young. Improper watering causes rot and leaf-tip burn.

Chinese Fan Palm

European Fan Palm
Chamaerops humilis
(ka-MEE-rops HEW-mi-lis)

Light: Bright light, but can be maintained for many weeks in lower light.

Water: Moderately moist soil. Water thoroughly when just the soil surface is dry to the touch. Do not allow plants to stand in water.

Temperature: Cool/Moderate – 60-70°F days and 55-65°F nights.

This palm is at its best when displayed in plenty of

European Fan Palm

space. Its growth habit is bushy and low. Segmented leaves on spiny stalks resemble a fan. If given enough water and light, it is an easy plant to care for. Watch for red spider mites.

Kentia Palm
Howea forsteriana
(HOW-ee-ah for-ster-ee-AY-nah)

Light: Indirect or bright, diffused light.

Water: Moderately moist soil. Water thoroughly when just the soil surface is dry to the touch. Do not allow plants to stand in water. Water sparingly in the winter.

Temperature: Moderate – 65-70°F days and 60-65°F nights.

The Kentia palm is easy to grow. Its graceful stems bear dark green, wide-spreading, leathery fronds, each growing successively larger than the next. Avoid overwatering. Prefers confined roots. Watch for red spider mites.

Kentia Palm

Lady Palm
Rhapis excelsa
(RAY-pis ek-SEL-suh)

The lady palm is easy to grow, but requires a little special attention. A native of southern China and a popular potted plant in Asia, the durable palm has bamboo-like canes and fan-like foliage. The thin stems are densely matted with coarse fibers, and the leathery, glossy leaves have 3-10 broad segments. Tolerates cooler conditions better than most palms. Lady Palms do well on porch or patio where they enjoy increased air circulation. Avoid overwatering. Watch for red spider mites.

Neanthe Bella Palm
Chamaedorea elegans 'Bella'
(kam-uh-DOR-ee-ah EL-uh-ganz)

Lady Palm

Light: Low light.

Water: Moderately moist soil. Water thoroughly when just the soil surface is dry to the touch. Do not allow plants to stand in water.

Temperature: Warm – 70-75°F days and 65-70°F nights.

Also known as dwarf parlor palm, the neanthe bella palm is easy to grow, but requires a little special attention. Native to Guatemalan mountain forests, the neanthe bella palm is a graceful slow-growing plant. It makes an elegant addition to low light areas in the home. Under ideal conditions, it may flower with reddish-orange blossoms. Common problems are yellowing leaves, root rot or browning tips due to improper watering. Watch for salt accumulation in the soil, red spider mites, scale and mealybugs.

Neanthe Bella Palm

Pigmy Date Palm
Phoenix roebelenii
(FEE-niks roe-beh-LIN-eye)

The pigmy date palm is easy to grow, but requires a little special attention. This palm has a thick trunk and spreading leaves. It is slow-growing and will not soon "take over" room space; however, mature specimens can reach up to 6 feet tall. Under watering will cause leaf-tip burn. Watch for red spider mites.

Pigmy Date Palm

Reed Palm
Chamaedorea seifrizii
(kam-uh-DOR-ee-ah see-FREE-zee-i)

The reed palm is easy to grow. This clustering palm exhibits graceful elegance. Common problems are yellowing leaves or browning tips due to improper watering. Overwatering will cause root rot. Watch for red spider mites, scale and mealybugs.

Reed Palm

popular plants

Paper White Narcissus
Narcissus tazetta 'Paper White'
(nar-SIS-is tah-ZET-ah)

Light: Indirect or bright, diffused light.

Water: Moderately moist soil. Water thoroughly when just the soil surface is dry to the touch. Do not allow plants to stand in water.

Temperature: Cool – 60-65°F days and 55-60°F nights.

The paper white narcissus is generally available from February through April. It bears bunches of small, fragrant white flowers with several clustered together on each stem. The blooming period is about 2 weeks.

Reflowering: Paper white narcissus is a tender bulb that cannot be reflowered once it has been forced into bloom.

Peperomia
Peperomia species
(pep-er-OH-mee-ah)

Light: Indirect or bright, diffused light.

Water: Maintain soil on the dry side. Drench soil thoroughly, then allow it to become moderately dry before watering again.

Temperature: Warm – 70-75°F days and 65-70°F nights.

The peperomia is easy to grow, but requires a little special attention. Peperomias are sturdy semi-succulent plants that will thrive under the dry conditions that will cause tip browning on other plants. Insects are seldom a problem. Avoid overwatering, especially at low temperatures or in high humidity. Overwatering causes crown rot and wilting, which encourages even more watering, aggravating the problem.

Persian Violet
Exacum affine   *Also known as Exacum*
(EK-sah-kum ah-FINE-ee)

Paper White Narcissus

Peperomia

Persian Violet

Light: Bright light.

Water: Moderately moist soil. Water thoroughly when just the soil surface is dry to the touch. Do not allow plants to stand in water.

Temperature: Moderate – 65-70°F days and 60-65°F nights.

The Persian Violet is generally available midsummer through fall. The bushy exacum offers a profusion of fragrant star-like flowers with prominent yellow stamens surrounded by waxy, oval leaves. The Persian Violet will flower 3-4 weeks as an indoor potted plant. The blossoms can range from pale violet to violet, blue, pink and white. The plant will continue to flower for 3-4 months if planted outdoors in a partly sunny location, if temperatures permit. Avoid overwatering and provide good drainage. Warm, humid, bright "greenhouse" conditions will prolong flowering indoors.

PHILODENDRON PLANTS

Light: Indirect or bright, diffused light.

Water: Moderately moist soil. Water thoroughly when just the soil surface is dry to the touch. Do not allow plants to stand in water.

Temperature: Warm – 70-75°F days and 65-70°F nights.

Unless otherwise indicated, most philodendrons prefer the above light, water and temperature requirements.

Angel Wing Philodendron
Philodendron 'Angel Wing'
(fil-oh-DEN-dron)

Light: Low light.

Water: Moderately moist soil. Water thoroughly when just the soil surface is dry to the touch. Do not allow plants to stand in water.

Temperature: Warm – 70-75°F days and 65-70°F nights.

Angel Wing Philodendron

Angel wing philodendron is easy to grow, but requires a little special attention. Philodendron are very popular because of their tremendous versatility. Extensive hybridization has developed a philodendron for every situation.

Angel wing philodendron is a climbing variety suitable for hanging baskets, 6-inch pots, ground cover or trellis. Do not overwater or overfertilize.

popular plants

Fiddle-Leaf Philodendron
Philodendron bipennifolium
(fil-oh-DEN-dron bih-pen-if-OH-lee-um)

The fiddle-leaf philodendron is easy to grow. Philodendron are among the most popular plants because of their tremendous versatility. This sturdy climber has large irregularly shaped leaves that somewhat resemble a fiddle. It's usually grown on a trellis.

Fiddle-Leafed
Philodendron

Heart-Leaf Philodendron
Philodendron scandens oxycardium
(fil-oh-DEN-dron SKAN-denz ox-ih-KAR-dee-um)

The heart-leaf philodendron is easy to grow. Philodendron are among the most popular plants because of their tremendous versatility. In nature, heart-leaf philodendron is a vigorous climbing vine but can be used as a ground cover. Shoots do not produce multiple branches when pinched, so multiple plants are necessary to keep it bushy. It tolerates low light quite well, but leaves will be smaller in very low light.

Heart-Leaf Philodendron

Pluto Philodendron
Philodendron 'Pluto'
(fil-oh-DEN-dron)

The Pluto Philodendron is easy to grow. Philodendron are among the most popular plants because of their tremendous versatility. This fast-growing variety is an excellent choice for interior use. It produces a rosette-like clump with a unique waffling of the leaves. New foliage is a characteristic bronze color as it emerges. Avoid cold temperatures.

Split-Leaf Philodendron
Monstera deliciosa
(mon-STEER-ah dee-lish-ee-OH-sah)

Light: Indirect or bright, diffused light.

Water: Moderately moist soil. Water thoroughly when just the soil surface is dry to the touch. Do not allow plants to stand in water.

Pluto Philodendron

Temperature: Warm – 70-75°F days and 65-70°F nights.

The easy-to-grow split-leaf philodendron gets its common name from the decorative perforations in its large, deeply lobed leaves. This handsome vine has clinging aerial roots and is most often grown on a pole support. Leaves tend to lose their perforations in low light or other poor growing conditions, and when they grow beyond their supports. Watch for scale and mealybugs.

Tree Philodendron
Philodendron selloum
(fil-oh-DEN-dron sell-OH-um)

Split-Leaf Philodendron

Light: Bright light, but can be maintained for many weeks in lower light.

Water: Moderately moist soil. Water thoroughly when just the soil surface is dry to the touch. Do not allow plants to stand in water.

Temperature: Warm – 70-75°F days and 65-70°F nights.

The tree philodendron is easy to grow. This wide-spreading, easy-care floor plant has striking, deeply lobed leaves that emerge in a rosette from its thick, slowly ascending trunk. Bright light will maintain deep lobing of the foliage.

Tree Philodendron

Piggy-Back Plant
Tolmiea menziesii
(tole-MEE-uh men-ZEE-see-eye)

Light: Indirect or bright, diffused light.

Water: Moderately moist soil. Water thoroughly when just the soil surface is dry to the touch. Do not allow plants to stand in water.

Temperature: Cool/Moderate – 60-70°F days and 55-65°F nights.

The piggy-back plant is easy to grow, but requires a little special attention. This unique plant bears baby plantlets at the base of its hairy leaves. A plantlet may be removed

Piggy-Back Plant

and put in soil to root, with the mother leaf covered with soil to anchor the new plant. Avoid direct sun and overwatering, as tender leaves may wilt and develop brown tips. Well-drained soil helps keep the leaves a healthy dark green. Watch for red spider mites and mealybugs.

Pilea

Pilea species
(pie-LEE-ah)

Light: Indirect or bright, diffused light.

Water: Moderately moist soil. Water thoroughly when just the soil surface is dry to the touch. Do not allow plants to stand in water.

Temperature: Warm – 70-75°F days and 65-70°F nights.

Pileas are easy to grow. They should be pinched regularly to help them keep their bushy shape. Pileas will tolerate typical home humidity conditions – dry air in winter and humid air in summer. They can be sensitive to insecticide damage. Take care not to overwater.

Pilea

Poinsettia

Euphorbia pulcherrima
(you-FORB-ee-ah pul-KER-ih-mah)

Light: Indirect or bright, diffused light.

Water: Moderately moist soil. Water thoroughly when just the soil surface is dry to the touch. Do not allow plants to stand in water.

Temperature: Moderate – 65-70°F days and 60-65°F nights.

This traditional holiday favorite is native to Mexico and is usually available in November and December. Poinsettias offer beautiful color ranging from red, pink and white to new peach, golden, and variegated varieties. Colorful bracts will last from 2-3 months. To delay flower bud drop and maintain the brightly colored

Poinsettia

bracts, keep your poinsettia in bright, diffused light with cooler night temperatures. Watch for whiteflies.

Reflowering: A reflowered poinsettia will not be as attractive as the original plant. Continue to care for the plant during the winter and early spring, reducing the amount of water in late winter. When the leaves drop, cut stems back by 1/3 - 1/2. Place in a cool indoor location until new leaves begin to emerge. At this point, repot and increase light and water. Then, after the danger of frost is past, place plant outdoors for better light. Return plant indoors in the fall before night temperatures fall to 40°F outdoors. To initiate the colorful bracts: October 1 to November 15, provide poinsettias with 14 hours of uninterrupted darkness followed by 10 hours of bright light each day. Once color bracts have begun to develop, the plant may be returned to normal indoor conditions. Please note that poinsettias are sensitive to even the smallest amount of light during the period of uninterrupted darkness, even street lights. Extra care is critical so that the darkness cycle is not broken.

POTHOS
Golden Pothos
Epipremnum aureum 'Wilcoxii'
(eh-pih-PREM-num are-EE-um)

Marble Queen Pothos
Epipremnum aureum 'Marble Queen'
(eh-pih-PREM-num are-EE-um)

Golden Pothos

Light: Indirect or bright, diffused light.

Water: Moderately moist soil. Water thoroughly when just the soil surface is dry to the touch. Do not allow plants to stand in water.

Temperature: Warm – 70-75°F days and 65-70°F nights.

Decorative pothos plants are easy to grow because they are tolerant of watering variations and resistant to pests. In low light they may lose some of their variegation and even take on a yellow or blackish discoloration. Shoots may not branch when pinched, so plants will never be bushy. However, each shoot can grow very long, cascading from ceiling to floor in a dramatic hanging basket.

Marble Queen Pothos

Prayer Plant

Prayer Plant
Maranta leuconeura 'Erythroneura'
(mah-RAN-tah loo-koh-NUR-ah air-ith-row-NUR-ah)

Light: Indirect or bright, diffused light.

Water: Moderately moist soil. Water thoroughly when just the soil surface is dry to the touch. Do not allow plants to stand in water.

Temperature: Warm – 70-75°F days and 65-70°F nights.

The prayer plant is moderately easy to grow, but has some special requirements for success. It gets its common name from the fact that its horizontal leaves fold up "in prayer" at night. The unusual oblong leaves have dark blotches, red veins and a purplish-red underside. High humidity is required to prevent browning of the leaf tips. Too-high light, excessive fertilizer, and high levels of fluoride and boron can also cause browning. When maranta plants begin to die, allow them to dry for 3-4 weeks, then begin watering, and new growth will appear. Watch for red spider mites and slugs, which are small snail-like organisms without shells.

Ribbon Plant

Ribbon Plant
Dracaena sanderiana
(drah-SEE-nah san-deer-ee-AY-nah)

Light: Indirect or bright, diffused light.

Water: Moderately moist soil. Water thoroughly when just the soil surface is dry to the touch. Do not allow plants to stand in water.

Temperature: Warm – 70-75°F days and 65-70°F nights.

Ribbon plants are easy to grow, but require a little special attention. Improper watering may cause excessive leaf-tip burn and leaf drop, though occasional dropping of leaves is normal. Root rot and scale may also be problems. Avoid excessive fertilizer or high levels of boron or fluoride, which can also cause leaf-tip burn.

RUBBER PLANTS
Ficus elastica
(FYE-kus ee-LAS-tih-kah)

Light: Indirect or bright, diffused light.

Water: Moderately moist soil. Water thoroughly when just the soil surface is dry to the touch. Do not allow plants to stand in water.

Temperature: Warm – 70-75°F days and 65-70°F nights.

Rubber Plant

Rubber plants are easy to grow and generally durable. They grow best in smaller containers, so repotting is seldom necessary. Rubber plants feature bright green leaves and a red growing tip. Plants can easily grow quite large with few problems, especially in a brighter location. Watch for red spider mites, scale and mealybugs.

Burgundy Rubber Plant
Ficus elastica 'Burgundy'
(FYE-kus ee-LAS-tih-kah)

This popular rubber plant has a slightly bronze-burgundy cast to its large shiny leaves. Under ideal conditions, it may grow very large. Bright light intensifies the red color.

SCHEFFLERA PLANTS
Amate Schefflera
Schefflera actinophylla 'Amate'
Formerly known as Brassaia actinophylla 'Amate'
(shef-LER-ah act-in-oh-FIE-lah)

Burgundy Rubber Plant

Light: Bright light, but can be maintained for many weeks in lower light.

Water: Maintain soil on the dry side. Drench soil thoroughly, then allow it to become moderately dry before watering again.

Temperature: Warm – 70-75°F days and 65-70°F nights.

Showy scheffleras are popular plants that thrive with minimal care, under proper conditions. Some leaf drop is normal as the plant adjusts to a new home, but this can

Amate Schefflera

also be a result of low light or improper watering. Low light causes cupped foliage that is pale between the veins. Avoid overwatering to prevent blackened leaves and dead leaf tips, which should be removed. Watch for red spider mites, scale and mealybugs.

Hawaiian Schefflera

Schefflera arboricola
Formerly known as Brassaia arboricola
(shef-LER-ah ar-bor-ih-COLE-ah)

The bushier Hawaiian schefflera has smaller leaves and avoids the long, leggy leaf stems of the typical schefflera. Hawaiian schefflera is more sensitive to overwatering. Prune regularly to keep plant shape symmetrical. Watch for red spider mites, scale and mealybugs.

Hawaiian Schefflera

Variegated Hawaiian Schefflera

Schefflera arboricola
Formerly known as Brassaia arboricola
(shef-LER-ah ar-bor-ih-COLE-ah)

Select Hawaiian schefflera varieties exhibit variegation patterns from yellowish gold to conspicuous ivory-white leaf margins. These attractive variegated cultivars are among the showiest of the species. Variegated varieties require more light to maintain the variegation.

Shamrock Plant

Oxalis oregana
(och-SOL-iss or-e-GA-nah)

Light: Indirect or bright, diffused light.

Water: Maintain soil on the dry side. Drench soil thoroughly, then allow it to become moderately dry before watering again.

Temperature: Cool/Moderate – 60-70°F days and 55-65°F nights.

Shamrock Plant

The shamrock plant is valued for its interesting "good luck" three-parted leaves and is available in March. The delicate white, pink or rose flowers are a bonus, lasting 2-3 weeks. Most varieties benefit from a rest period of several months. After blooming, decrease watering and temperature (50-60°F). Cut back foliage or allow it to die down. Repotting and division of overgrown plants should be done at this time. Resuming regular watering, temperature and fertilization will start your shamrock plant on its way to blooming again.

SPATHIPHYLLUM PLANTS

Light: Low light.

Water: Moderately moist soil. Water thoroughly when just the soil surface is dry to the touch. Do not allow plants to stand in water.

Variegated Hawaiian Schefflera

Temperature: Warm – 70-75°F days and 65-70°F nights.

Spathiphyllum is easy to grow and generally not troubled by any major insects. Plants wilt quickly when under watered, and leaf edges will turn brown. Excess salts (or fertilizer) will also cause brown leaf edges. Avoid combinations of high temperatures and dry soil at the same time, or cold temperatures and wet soil at the same time.

Mauna Loa Spathiphyllum
Spathiphyllum 'Mauna Loa'
Also known as White Flag or Peace Lily
(spath-if-EYE-lum)

Mauna Loa will reach a mature height of 4-5 feet. The broad, glossy leaves exhibit an obvious bold texture with long leaf stems. Taller spathiphyllum make excellent floor plants.

Mauna Loa Spathiphyllum

Mauna Loa Supreme Spathiphyllum
Spathiphyllum 'Mauna Loa Supreme'
Also known as White Flag or Peace Lily
(spath-if-EYE-lum)

Mauna Loa Supreme is a medium-sized spathiphyllum. This plant will grow to a height of about 3 feet. It is a more symmetrical plant with leaf stems about half the length of the Mauna Loa variety.

Mauna Loa Supreme Spathiphyllum

Wallis Spathiphyllum

Wallis Spathiphyllum

Spathiphyllum 'Wallisii'
Also known as White Flag or Peace Lily
(spath-if-EYE-lum)

This is a small, compact, vigorous spathiphyllum that matures to a height of 12 inches. It exhibits delicate 3-inch blooms.

Snake Plant

Sansevieria trifasciata
Also known as Mother-in-Law's Tongue
(san-zuh-VEER-ee-uh try-fash-ee-AY-tah)

Light: Low light.

Water: Maintain soil on the dry side. Drench soil thoroughly, then allow it to become moderately dry before watering again.

Temperature: Warm – 70-75°F days and 65-70°F nights.

Snake Plant

The easy-to-grow snake plant has tough green sword-shaped leaves with yellow banded margins. Noted for its ability to withstand abuse, the snake plant is not generally vulnerable to insects. It can survive adverse growing conditions, except overwatering, which causes rot. Under extended poor conditions, snake plants will grow longer and thinner. Under good conditions, it may reward you with a cluster of fragrant flowers.

Spider Plant

Chlorophytum comosum 'Variegata'
(klor-oh-FYE-tum koh-MOH-sum)

Light: Indirect or bright, diffused light.

Water: Moderately moist soil. Water thoroughly when just the soil surface is dry to the touch. Do not allow plants to stand in water.

Temperature: Moderate – 65-70°F days and 60-65°F nights.

Spider Plant

The easy-to-grow spider plant is popular because of the little plantlets that form on long, flowering stalks that develop from the center of the plant. These "spiders" may be left dangling or removed and repotted to start new plants. Browning of the leaf tips may be a problem caused by dry soil, overfertilization, low light, fluoride salts or excess boron. Watch for red spider mites and provide good drainage.

Swedish Ivy
Plectranthus species
(plek-TRANTH-us)

Swedish Ivy

Light: Indirect or bright, diffused light.

Water: Moderately moist soil. Water thoroughly when just the soil surface is dry to the touch. Do not allow plants to stand in water.

Temperature: Warm – 70-75°F days and 65-70°F nights.

Swedish ivy is fast growing, easy to care for, and is handsome in a hanging container. Because it roots quickly in water, it is easy to generate many new plants in a short time. They are not generally troubled by insects; however, overwatering will cause bottom leaves to yellow and drop. Tolerates bright light.

Tahitian Bridal Veil
Gibasis geniculata
(je-BAY-sis jen-IK-u-lah-ta)

Tahitian Bridal Veil

Light: Indirect or bright, diffused light.

Water: Maintain soil on the dry side. Drench soil thoroughly, then allow it to become moderately dry before watering again.

Temperature: Moderate – 65-70°F days and 60-65°F nights.

The Tahitian bridal veil is easy to grow. It is a vigorous hanging plant that stays bushy and more attractive if pruned regularly. The resulting cuttings root easily in rooting medium or in water. This plant can be grown indefinitely in water. In soil, however, it is sensitive to overwatering as well as to red spider mites. Tiny olive-green leaves and white flowers cascade in a decorative veil from this dainty hanging plant. Flowering is more profuse in high light.

Thanksgiving Cactus
Schlumbergera truncatus
(shlum-BER-jer-ah trung-KAY-tahs)

Light: Indirect or bright, diffused light.

Water: Moderately moist soil. Water thoroughly when just the soil surface is dry to the touch. Do not allow plants to stand in water.

Temperature: Cool/Moderate – 60-70°F days and 55-65°F nights.

Thanksgiving cactus, also known as Christmas cactus or holiday cactus, have showy flowers and flattened, spiny joints. This makes it an interesting houseplant. Thanksgiving cactus are generally available from October through December. They bloom from 4-8 weeks in a wide range of colors including red, pink, white, salmon, and bicolors. They prefer a well-drained, rich soil. This cactus is often sold as Christmas cactus although the true Christmas cactus has no spines on the joints. Bud drop can be caused by overwatering, under watering, low light, night temperatures over 60°F or sudden temperature changes.

Reflowering: Place the plant in continuous, uninterrupted darkness for 14 hours daily at night temperatures of 60°F and day temperatures not over 65°F during October and November. Then bring the cactus into a bright area where it will continue to develop and flower.

Thanksgiving Cactus

Tulip
Tulipa cultivars
(TOO-lip-ah)

Light: Indirect or bright, diffused light.

Water: Moderately moist soil. Water thoroughly when just the soil surface is dry to the touch. Do not allow plants to stand in water.

Temperature: Cool – 60-65°F days and 55-60°F nights.

Tulip

Tulip plants are generally available from January through early May. They are grown in a range of colors including white, cream, yellow, orange, red, pink, lavender, purple, and bicolors. Blossoms will last from 1-2 weeks. Cool night temperatures (50-60°F) will prolong flowering indoors. Although tulips have become associated with the Netherlands, they originated in Asia Minor. They have been cultivated in the West for over 400 years, and many diverse varieties have been developed.

Reflowering: Bulbs will not reflower indoors once they have been forced out of season, but may be planted outdoors. Remove the flowers after they have faded, keep the plant in its cool night location and continue watering until the foliage matures. In late spring, plant it in the garden. It will bloom in 1 or 2 years during its normal blooming season.

Wandering Jew
Tradescantia zebrina
Formerly known as Zebrina pendula
(trad-es-KAN-tee-ah zee-BRY-nah)

Light: Indirect or bright, diffused light.

Water: Moderately moist soil. Water thoroughly when just the soil surface is dry to the touch. Do not allow plants to stand in water.

Temperature: Moderate/Warm – 65-75°F days and 60-70°F nights.

Wandering Jew

Wandering Jew is easy to grow. Its striped leaves range from deep green to purple with two silver bands and have a purple underside. In low light, the green color dominates; in high light, the purple increases. Regular pinching helps keep the plant bushy and encourages branching. Cuttings root easily at leaf joints; root them in water or rooting medium.

Weeping Fig
Ficus benjamina
(FYE-kus ben-jam-EE-nah)

Light: Indirect or bright, diffused light.

Water: Moderately moist soil. Water thoroughly when just the soil surface is dry to the touch. Do not allow plants to stand in water.

Temperature: Warm – 70-75°F days and 65-70°F nights.

Weeping Fig

The weeping fig is easy to grow, but requires a little special attention. Ficus are generally durable and grow best in smaller containers, so repotting is seldom necessary. Once established in a good location in a home or office, the weeping fig will last for years. This artistic tree displays glossy, deep green leaves, each with a gentle twist. It has a tendency to drop some of its leaves whenever it changes environment or experiences a draft. Weeping figs are sensitive to both insufficient light and lack of water. Loss of yellow leaves and leaf-tip burn are due to inconsistent watering. An overall lack of growth and a decrease in size of new leaves are good indicators of insufficient light. Watch for red spider mites and mealybugs.

Spineless Yucca
Yucca elephantipes
(yah-KAH el-ee-fan-TIPES)

Variegated Spineless Yucca
Yucca elephantipes 'Variegata'
(yah-KAH el-ee-fan-TIPES)

Light: Bright light.

Water: Moderately moist soil. Water thoroughly when just the soil surface is dry to the touch. Do not allow plants to stand in water.

Temperature: Cool/Moderate – 60-70°F days and 55-65°F nights.

Spineless yucca can be a little challenging to grow but well worth the effort. Reduce water in winter months if the plant is kept at a low temperature. It can be moved outdoors during the summer to a sunny location. Few problems with diseases and insects. Avoid overwatering.

Spineless Yucca

Variegated Spineless
Yucca

Zebra Plant

Aphelandra squarrosa
(a-fuh-LAN-drah square-OH-sah)

Light: Indirect or bright, diffused light.

Water: Moderately moist soil. Water thoroughly when just the soil surface is dry to the touch. Do not allow plants to stand in water.

Temperature: Warm – 70-75°F days and 65-70°F nights.

Zebra Plant

Zebra plant is available all year. Native to Brazil, this plant is a challenge to grow, but its dramatic striped foliage and yellow flower spikes are well worth the extra effort. The flower spikes can last 3-5 weeks. The zebra plant is particular about its care. It should be kept constantly moist; if it wilts even once, foliage will dry and fall. It requires a rich soil and high humidity (50-60%). Zebra plant is quite difficult to maintain in flower, but the foliage is very attractive on its own. Flowering may be encouraged by high light intensity. Watch for aphids, mealybugs and whiteflies.

plant problems

Insects are the most serious problem in any indoor plant environment. They thrive in a warm, dry atmosphere and can quickly get out of control unless plants are checked carefully at regular intervals. The five insects that cause major damage to foliage and flowering plants are aphids, mealybugs, scale, two-spotted spider mites and whiteflies. Fungus gnats, leaf miners and thrips can cause minor damage.

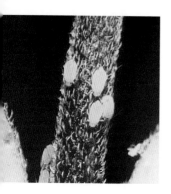

Aphids

INSECT PESTS

A major part of insect control in any situation is prevention. Whether you have one plant or hundreds, the following precautionarys will aid in preventing insect infestations.

1. Inspect the leaves and stems for insects on any new plants before placing them with existing plants.

2. If repotting is necessary, use only clean, disinfected pots and sterilized soil.

3. Minimize handling plants to avoid transferring insects from one plant to another. After handling infested plants, wash hands and sterilize tools.

4. Keep plant leaves clean and dusted so they can absorb all available light.

Fungus Gnat

Even when the best prevention techniques have been used, insect populations may build up. Many light infestations can be controlled with non-chemical treatments. Although these treatments will not completely control the infestation, they will reduce the insect population. Repeat the process as population builds up.

1. Light infestations of aphids and mealybugs may be controlled with rubbing alcohol, either by using cotton swabs and rubbing it on the insects, or by spraying it on.

2. Mineral oil will control light infestations of scale, if applied at the right stage of insect growth.

3. A soapy water treatment using 1 teaspoon of non-detergent household soap in 1 gallon of water may be effective against smaller insects. Mist with warm

Mealybugs

water to rinse. Repeating this treatment two or three times at five-day intervals will usually interrupt the insects' life cycle.

Severely infested plants can be treated with pyrethrum, rotenone, dicofol, nicotine and malathion if good ventilation is provided. These chemicals are available under different trade names. Check pesticide labels to see what you are buying, then follow the directions carefully.

Sometimes insect population growth or the damage caused by insects can be so great that you cannot save the plant. It should be destroyed so it does not contaminate other plants.

Mineral oil is a deterrent to some pests

Aphids

Aphids are tiny sucking insects about 1/8" long. They may be winged or non-winged and can be black, red, orange, green, yellow, or tan in color. Ants can play a part in the migration of aphids from one plant to another; therefore, control sometimes depends on the elimination of ants. Damaged plants lose their green color and appear stunted, distorted, or curled. Aphids secrete honeydew, which gives the plant a shiny appearance and is the basis for the growth of black, sooty mold.

Fungus Gnats

Fungus gnats are small, slender, black flies. They are commonly found in highly organic soils or unsterilized soil and rarely cause damage to plants. If damage does occur, feeder roots, larger roots, seedlings and succulent stems are chewed and injured.

Mealybugs

Mealybugs are slender, flat insects covered by a waxy substance. As they mature, they form a white, cottony mass. Adult mealybugs inhabit cracks and crevices of buds, stems, and branches. They weaken and slow growth of infested plants. Mealybugs also secrete honeydew.

Scale

Scale insects are about 1/4" long. The scale is actually a covering that serves to protect the insect. Females lay

Scale

eggs under the protective covering. When the young hatch, they are transparent, oval and flat. The first growth stage is the "crawler." It's at this stage that scale are most susceptible to insecticides. Look for scale along leaf veins and on stems. Infested plants exhibit poor growth and stunting.

Thrips

Spider Mites

Spider mites produce fine webs (like spiders) on the undersides of plant leaves. The web protects both the mites and their eggs. Mites are wingless and usually pale yellow to red in color. Mite damage first appears as whitish or yellowish speckled areas. Leaves may take on a bronze appearance and may die and fall from the plant. Warm, dry conditions favor mite infestations. Mites can be very hard to control because they reproduce rapidly in high temperatures, building up large populations quickly, and they can develop a tolerance to miticides.

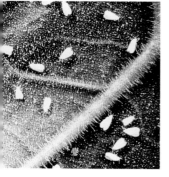

Whiteflies

Thrips

Female thrips insert their eggs into host tissue. One week later the eggs hatch, and within two to four weeks their life cycle is completed. Thrips suck plant juices and in doing so, rasp and shred the leaf. The injured plant turns white and shows signs of black secretions. Thrips are usually found in blossoms and in the axils of leaves.

Whiteflies

Whiteflies are tiny, snow-white insects. Adult females can lay up to 100 crescent-shaped eggs per month on the underside of leaves. Whiteflies will breed continuously in interior environments, thereby creating large populations rapidly. Infested plants become weak, deformed and pale, and eventually die. Whiteflies secrete honeydew.

PLANT DISEASES

Plant disease is dependent on three factors: the presence of a susceptible host, the pathogen, and environmental conditions conducive to disease development. All of these factors must be present for disease to occur. If any of these factors can be modified or eliminated, the incidence of plant disease can be reduced or eliminated. Plant disease is caused by three major groups of organisms: fungi, bacteria and viruses.

Fungi

Warm temperatures and high moisture levels favor the growth of fungi. They penetrate host tissue either directly or by means of natural openings like leaf pores, or through wounds. The fungus then begins to digest plant tissue.

Bacteria

Bacteria are microscopic, primitive plants that penetrate the host through wounds or natural plant openings. Growth of bacteria is encouraged by warm temperatures and high moisture levels.

Viruses

Viruses are infectious nucleoproteins that enter the host through wounds or natural openings, usually with the assistance of some other agent such as an insect. Controlling the agent that spreads the pathogen is the only way to control a virus; sprays will not help.

Control of Diseases

The environment in which a plant is growing plays a very large part in the establishment of any disease. The following practices will help reduce the likelihood of plant disease.

1. Keep foliage dry to reduce the incidence of foliage leaf spots.
2. Remove infected tissues (where possible) to reduce the spread of disease to unaffected tissues or plants.
3. Disinfect implements – such as scissors, pruning shears, dust rags, sponges – and hands before moving from a diseased plant to a healthy one.

Fungal Leaf Spot on a dieffenbachia

4. Clean and disinfect all plants before potting them, and use clean potting media.

COMMON DISEASES
Fungal Leaf Spot

Many types of fungal leaf spot may attack foliage plants. They begin as a small, papery lesion that is gray to dark brown in color. As the lesion spreads, it develops a bull's-eye surrounded by a halo.

Bacterial Leaf Spot and Stem Rot

Bacterial infections appear as water-soaked areas, often greasy-looking and surrounded by a halo. Bacterial soft rot (leaves and stems) occurs quickly, creating mushy, foul-smelling tissue.

Root Rot

These diseases are caused by fungi of the genus Pythium, Phytophthora, or Rhizoctonia. Pythium and Phytophthora cause root rot. Roots turn mushy and brown to black in color. Development of these fungi is encouraged by warm soil and an abundance of water. Rhizoctonia causes damping-off of seedlings. It attacks older foliage plants at the soil line, producing dry, reddish-brown leaves.

Botrytis Blight

Botrytis blight appears as a gray mold in situations of high humidity and poor air circulation. In most stages it appears furry and releases a fine dust when disturbed. Botrytis blight is common on flowering plants.

GENERAL PLANT PROBLEMS

Plants will vary in their appearance, and some problems are not easily diagnosed. When examining a plant, begin by determining which part is affected. The soil will also provide clues. To help you evaluate plant problems, use this table of specific problems, symptoms and their probable causes.

Whole Plant Affected

Plant is stunted or not growing. The leaves are green and appear healthy, but there is little or no new growth.
Possible causes:

- Insufficent light
- Overwatering
- Poor soil mix
- Overfertilization
- Insects or disease
- Potbound
- Improper repotting
- Improper temperature

The entire plant is wilted and has drooping leaves.
Possible causes:

- Improper watering
- Overfertilization
- Poor soil mix
- Disease
- Improper repotting
- Drafts
- Improper temperature
- Stem broken or injured

Poor new growth – pale leaves, spindly growth.

Possible causes:

- Low light
- Too-high temperature
- Underfertilization

Slow growth even under optimum care conditions. Soil dries out quickly, and more frequent watering is required. Roots growing through drainage holes.
Possible causes:

- Potbound

Stems and Branches Affected

Stems are discolored (water-soaked) and mushy or rotten.
Possible causes:

- Overwatering
- Disease (stem rot)
- Poor soil mix

The branches die back.
Possible causes:

- Disease
- Insects
- Severe light burn

The lower stem is discolored or shows signs of decay or rotting.
Possible causes:

- Overwatering
- Disease

Portions of the stem have been chewed

away; there are holes, stripping, or discoloration.
Possible causes:
- Pets
- Insects feeding on stems

There are white strands of cottony material on lower
stem.
Possible causes:
- Insects
- Disease (mildew or mold)

Leaves Affected

The lower leaves are turning yellow and falling off.
Possible causes:
- Overwatering
- Insufficient light
- High temperature
- Normal leaf drop
- Low humidity
- Insects

The lower leaves are green, but are falling off.
Possible causes:
- Environmental change
- Drafts
- Physical removal by people or pets

There is general leaf drop.
Possible causes:
- Environmental change
- Under watering
- Transplant shock
- Insects
- Lack of pruning: dense growth is shading
  out inner leaves

Leaf edges and tips are turning brown or have a
scorched appearance.
Possible causes:
- Under watering
- Overfertilization
- Low humidity

- Sun scorch
- Drafts
- Fluoride toxicity
- Contact with hot or cold surface

The leaves have a white powdery or cottony
growth on them.
Possible causes:
- Insects
- Disease (mildew)
- Salts from hard water

Loss of variegation (variegated plants turn all green).
Possible causes:
- Low light

Leaves are rotting (have brown or black spots).
Possible causes:
- Disease (leaf spot)
- Improper watering
- Insects
- Sun scorch
- Spray injury
- Leaf-shine damage
- Water spots on leaves

Leaves are distorted, curled or cupped.
Possible causes:
- Insect damage
- Under watering
- Poor light
- Pot-bound
- Spray damage
- Low humidity

Yellow leaves in upper part of plant.
Possible causes:
- Damaged roots
- Iron deficiency

Yellow leaves in middle to lower part of plant.
Possible causes:
- Overwatering
- Cold drafts
- Low humidity
- Underfertilization

Brown edges or spots on leaves.
Possible causes:
- Hot, dry air
- Sun scorch
- Pests or disease
- Too cold

Brown leaves.
Possible causes:
- Lack of water
- Improper temperature
- Underfertilization

Flowers Affected

Buds and flowers wilt, turn brown and drop off.
Possible causes:
- Lack of water
- Lack of humidity

Roots Affected

Roots are brown and mushy; rotting.
Possible causes:
- Overwatering
- Too-heavy soil

Roots are brown and dry.
Possible causes:
- Overfertilization
- Under watering

plant problems

Soil Condition Affected

The soil area has very fine, white-crusted matter on it.
Possible causes:
- Improper watering (salt buildup)

The soil shows signs of white strands of cottony material.
Possible causes:
- Disease (mold or mildew)

There are small, black flies on the soil.
Possible causes:
- Insects (fungus gnats)

There are little worms in the soil.
Possible causes:
- Insects (larvae of fungus gnats)

Guide for Determining Plant Problems

As you can see, there are many possible causes for most plant problems. Listed below are some questions you can ask yourself as you try to identify the source of the problem. Remember that more than half the problems are cultural in origin (improper water, light, etc.). The next most likely cause would be pests, and the least likely would be disease. If you cannot successfully identify the problem, consult your local plant professional for help.

Do you know what kind of plant it is? Care conditions vary among different types of plants. Some are more susceptible to certain pests than others.

How long have you had it? A recently acquired plant, for example, may be experiencing shock from a sudden change of light, temperature, or watering. An older plant may be root-bound and need to be repotted.

When did you first observe the problem? Can it be tied to other factors, such as moving the plant, fertilizing, use of pesticides, etc.?

What does the plant look like? Describe the problem or symptoms you have observed. What portion of the plant shows the symptoms?
- Is there wilting?
- Are leaves yellow, brown, curled, spotted or marked?
- Are stems firm or soft? Do they show signs of disease or insects?
- Are roots growing out through drainage holes? Do roots show signs of rot when plant is removed from the pot?
- Any other observations?

What are the plant's environmental conditions?
- Is it alone or in a group? Is it the only plant affected or are others affected also?
- Does the same problem occur in other locations or only in one area?
- What kind of light does the plant receive? Natural light? Artificial light – incandescent, fluorescent, special "grow" light? Low, medium or high light?
- What are the soil and container conditions? Is soil dry, moist or wet? What are the watering habits? What kind of pot – clay, ceramic, plastic? Is there a drainage hole? Is the container too large or too small? What type of soil is used? What is the pH level?
- What are air, humidity and temperature conditions? Is there active air movement? Is it dry or humid? What are the day and night temperatures? Has the plant been subject to temperature extremes? Is there a possibility of gases in the air?

What kind of care program do you have for the plant?
- What is the type and frequency of fertilizer or pesticide use?
- Watering frequency? Type of water? Temperature of water? Misting?
- Has plant been moved recently?
- Has plant been checked for insects or disease?

Have there been any unusual circumstances or accidents? Has the family pet been munching on the leaves? Has the plant been tipped over? Is it on a heating unit or in front of an air conditioner? Has it been exposed to cold air drafts?

Notes

_____

_____

_____

_____

index

common name index

Common Name Index

Common Name Index

Common Name Index

botanical name index

Botanical Name Index

botanical name index

Botanical Name Index

Botanical Name Index

Inquiries should be addressed to:
The John Henry Company
P.O. Box 17099
5800 W. Grand River Ave.
Lansing, MI 48901-7099

Library of Congress
Catalog Card Number: 95-076757
ISBN 0-9630431-1-0

Printed, published and distributed by
The John Henry Company, Lansing, MI